The Three Sisters

A PLAY BY

Anton Chekhov

ADAPTED BY

David Mamet

FROM A LITERAL TRANSLATION BY
VLADA CHERNOMORDIK

GROVE WEIDENFELD
New York

Published by Grove Weidenfeld
A division of Grove Press, Inc.
841 Broadway
New York, NY 10003-4793

Published in Canada by General Publishing Company, Ltd.

Library of Congress Cataloging-in-Publication Data

Chekhov, Anton Pavlovich, 1860–1904.
[Tri sestry.   English]
Three sisters : a play / by Anton Chekhov ; adapted by David Mamet from a literal translation by Vlada Chernomordik. — 1st ed.
p.   cm.
Translation of: Tri sestry.
ISBN 0-8021-3276-6 (alk. paper)
I. Mamet, David.   II. Chernomordik, Vlada.   III. Title.
pG3456.T8C48   1990
891.72'3—dc20   91-12802
CIP

Manufactured in the United States of America

Printed on acid-free paper

Designed by Irving Perkins Associates

First Edition 1991
First Evergreen Edition 1991

3   5   7   9   10   8   6   4   2

David Mamet's adaptation of *The Three Sisters* was first produced by the Atlantic Theater Company in Burlington, Vermont, August 1990. The production was directed by W. H. Macy, with the following cast:

OLGA SERGEYEVNA	Melissa Bruder
IRINA SERGEYEVNA	Mary McCann
MASHA SERGEYEVNA	Felicity Huffman
IVAN ROMANOVICH CHEBUTYKIN	Mike Nussbaum
NIKOLAI LVOVICH TUZENBACH	Todd Weeks
VASSILY VASSILYEVICH SOLYONY	Clark Gregg
ANFISA	Marge Kotlisky
FERAPONT	Paul Guare
ALEXANDR IGNATYEVICH VERSHININ	Jordan Lage
ANDREI SERGEYEVICH PROZOROFF	Neil Pepe
FYODOR ILYCH KULYGIN	Steven Goldstein
NATALYA IVANOVNA	Sarah Eckhardt
ALEXI PETROVICH FEDOTIK	Robert Bella
VLADIMIR KARLOVICH RODE	Scott Zigler
MAID	Robin Spielberg

The Three Sisters was subsequently produced by the Philadelphia Festival Theater for New Plays in collaboration with the Atlantic Theater Company, Annenberg Center, January–February 1991. The director and cast were the same as that of the Atlantic Theater Company production, except for the following cast changes:

IVAN ROMANOVICH CHEBUTYKIN	William Duff Griffin
ANFISA	Barbara Winters Pinto
FERAPONT	Andrew B. McCosker

Characters

ANDREI SERGEYEVICH PROZOROFF
NATALYA IVANOVNA, his fiancée, afterward his wife.
OLGA ⎫
MASHA ⎬ his sisters.
IRINA ⎭
FYODOR ILYCH KULYGIN, a high-school teacher, husband
    of MASHA.
LIEUTENANT COLONEL ALEXANDR IGNATYEVICH VERSHININ,
    battery commander.
BARON NIKOLAI LVOVICH TUZENBACH, lieutenant.
VASSILY VASSILYEVICH SOLYONY, captain.
IVAN ROMANOVICH CHEBUTYKIN, army doctor.
ALEXI PETROVICH FEDOTIK, second lieutenant.
VLADIMIR KARLOVICH RODE, second lieutenant.
FERAPONT, an old porter from the District Board.
ANFISA, the nanny, an old woman of eighty.

SCENE

The action takes place in a provincial town.

The Three Sisters

Act I

The Prozoroffs' House—a parlor. Mid-day. The table is being set for breakfast.

OLGA, IRINA, *and* MASHA.

OLGA: Well. I'm going to tell you. It's funny the way time does pass. Here we are. The same day. One year later. Irina. And the anniversaries. Irina's birthday and the day of Father's death. Which now will always be linked. And it snowed then. It was bitter cold, I thought that I would not survive it, you lay in a faint. And one year has passed and we can remember it with ease. You in a white dress, your face shining. (*The clock strikes.*) And the clock was striking then, it's striking *now*. (*Pause.*) When we went to the cemetery. To the martial music. In honor of our father. And the ceremonial salutes. Guns for a general. Commanded a brigade. Yet so few mourners. Didn't you think? Walking. Heavy rain and snow.

IRINA: Must you?

(CHEBUTYKIN, TUZENBACH, *and* SOLYONY *can be seen in the reception room.*)

1

OLGA: But today. Mmm. Today it is warm. We keep the windows open though the birches still are closed. You know. Eleven years ago. When we left Moscow. (*Pause.*) Eleven years ago. When he was given the brigade. When we left Moscow. At this time. The beginning of May, I remember it. As *so* warm. As if it were yesterday. Do you know—when I woke this morning, I saw the spring light. My soul responded to that light. As that light which we'd left, and I was filled with *passion*. To be back again.

CHEBUTYKIN: . . . in *Hell* . . .

TUZENBACH: It's garbage, what it is.

(MASHA *whistles a song quietly.*)

OLGA: Masha. Please don't whistle. *Please.*

MASHA: . . . Don't whistle?

OLGA: Please. My head is splitting, I've grown old *working*, and I'm sorry if I seem to *carp*, but I need some *quiet*, you know . . . ?

MASHA: . . . some quiet.

OLGA: . . . and a rest. From the *gymnasium* and *lessons* and four years of teaching constantly until I'm going to die because each lesson is a cup of my blood drained. Eh? And only one thought in my heart.

IRINA: To write a close to everything here and to go to Moscow.

OLGA: Yes. That's right. (*Pause.*) That's right. As soon as possible.

(CHEBUTYKIN *and* TUZENBACH *laugh offstage.*)

IRINA: And Brother to get his diploma and move off, the sole remainder being Masha.

OLGA: Who will come to Moscow the entire summer. Every year.

IRINA: Then, God grant, everything will come 'round right.

OLGA: Amen.

IRINA: A lovely day today.

OLGA: Yes, it is.

IRINA: My soul feels so light—do you know? This morning? I remembered that it was my birthday? And I felt such joy. And such *thoughts* moving me—of *Mama*.

OLGA: . . . Rest in peace.

IRINA: Rest in peace . . . and . . . such wonderful thoughts —such *memories* . . .

OLGA: Oh, darling. You are so beautiful today. You are radiant. Masha is shining, Andrei himself would look good, only he's gotten so terribly fat, hasn't he?

MASHA: Yes.

OLGA: Doesn't suit him.

MASHA: No.

OLGA: But I . . .

MASHA: . . . that's right . . .

OLGA: . . . I have grown old. I have grown very old. And thin—from being cross all of the time . . . with the girls at the gymnasium. Of whom I today am free. (*Pause.*) Thank God. And make me younger. I feel younger

today. I do. And it all is God—I know it. Life is good. It
. . . Life all flows from God, and I am only twenty-eight
years old. And I don't have a bad life . . .

MASHA: . . . no.

OLGA: Only it seems. If I were *married* . . . in love with my
husband. Married, do you know . . . ?

TUZENBACH (*to* SOLYONY): What garbage, excuse me, I'm
sick of listening to you. (*Entering parlor.*) Forgot to *in-
form* you that our new battery commander, Vershinin,
will today be paying you a visit.

OLGA: Very glad.

IRINA: Is he old?

TUZENBACH: Not overly. Forty-five? Forty? Seems a decent
sort. Not stupid. Not at all. Talks a bit, though . . .

IRINA: An interesting man?

TUZENBACH: As I said. Not bad. Got a wife, mother-in-
law—two girls. Second marriage. Everywhere he goes
he tells you that he's got a wife and the two girls. He'll
say it to you, too. You watch him. And his wife's a piece
of work. Long schoolgirl braid; she's given to philosophy and "*says*" things, don't'cha know. And tries to
take her wee life now and then. We think to spite her
husband. Another man'd ditch 'er. *I* would—he bears it
and complains.

SOLYONY (*entering with* CHEBUTYKIN): One arm, I can lift
fifty pounds. Eh? With *two* arms, I can lift . . . five times
that. We can conclude that two people, that the
strength of two, is not twice but *three* times, perhaps
more, more . . .

CHEBUTYKIN (*reading a newspaper*): For *hair* loss . . . two parts *naphthalene* . . . to . . . what is this? To ten parts alcohol. Dissolve. And apply daily . . . *Note* it! Do we note it? I was saying . . . putcher cork into your bottle and you take your Small Glass Tube. Alright—a tiny pinch of common or everyday *alum* . . .

IRINA: Ivan *Romanych* . . . my dear *Romanych* . . .

CHEBUTYKIN: Yes, my fount of joy?

IRINA: Why am I so completely happy today . . . ?

CHEBUTYKIN: Tell me . . .

IRINA: I am borne by sails. Beneath the softest sky. White birds overhead, flying by me . . . why . . . ?

CHEBUTYKIN (*kissing her hands*): The lovely birds of white . . .

IRINA: When I got up today. I got up and washed, and I got up and it seemed clear to me. Everything in the world. It was all clear to me—the way one ought to live. My dear Ivan Romanych—shall I tell you?

CHEBUTYKIN: Yes.

IRINA: By toil. We must live by toil. By the sweat of our brow. Each person must. This is the whole meaning of life. All happiness. *All* happiness. That laborer, do you see, up at dawn—who pounds stones in the streets, a shepherd, a, a *teacher*—in the cold dark—lighting the stove—who works with *children*. A . . . a railroad engineer . . . a, any, don't you see. Better to be a beast, an ox, a dray horse pulling in the street—*as long as one works*—than to be a woman of our class, rising at noon, to have her coffee brought her and to lie around, to spend two hours dressing . . . the revolving horror of a life with no work in it—I love to work. Ivan Romanych, as a parched man in the desert longs for water, I long to work. And if I do *not* work, Ivan Romanych, if I do not find that work, and toil—deny me your friendship— discard me. (*Pause.*) Reject me.

CHEBUTYKIN (*tenderly*): I swear it.

IRINA: *Will* you . . . ?

CHEBUTYKIN: Yes. Yes.

OLGA: Father trained us to get up at seven. So Irina now rises at seven, lies in bed til nine—her face screwed up, "thinking." About things . . .

IRINA: No, no, you see, you are used to thinking of me as a little girl, and so you find it strange if I seem serious.

OLGA: Mmm.

IRINA: I'm twenty years *old* . . .

TUZENBACH: No, it's not strange to long for labor. (*Sighs.*) *Oh*, God . . . no, I understand it—I, if I may speak of myself, haven't worked a day in my life. Born in Petersburg—a city of the cold and idle, into a family that knew neither worry nor work—I'd come home, I remember, I'd come home from military school, the footman, he would pull my boots off. No, I would be "acting up," you know, with him, I would treat him with insolence and my mother would *beam*. She'd look on me with benevolence, and of course, I was amazed when I found others who reacted differently. They shielded me, they *hid* me from the fact of labor. But they did not serve me, neither did they *protect* me—because the time has come—the juggernaut is bearing down upon us. And that storm is brooding. Brooding. Very near—preparing to fall upon us, that powerful storm, that healthy storm which will cleanse from our society the sloth, the indifference. The scorn of labor, the boredom—*I* shall work, not only shall *I* work—in twenty-five, in thirty years, we *all* shall work. Each person shall work. Every one.

CHEBUTYKIN: I won't work.

TUZENBACH: You don't count.

SOLYONY: In twenty-five years you'll be dead—thank God—two, three more years, you'll die of a stroke, or I'll, I don't know, I'll fly off the handle one day, and jump up and shoot you dead.

CHEBUTYKIN: Yes. Literally true—I've never done a thing—not one—never lifted a finger, any single thing could be called work. Not since I left the university, and never read a book. Read the newspapers. (*Takes out a newspaper.*) Look here, there is a, for example, fellow called *Dobroliudov,* writer—*but*—what he's been *writing,* I could not tell you—*God* only knows— (*Sound of knocking.*) Uh . . . huh . . . calling me downstairs. Yes. Someone there for me—back presently. Wait—eh? (*Exits.*)

IRINA: Something occurred to him.

TUZENBACH: It seems. Left rather pensive.

IRINA: Mmm.

TUZENBACH: You watch—he'll come back and bring you up some "offering."

IRINA: How distasteful.

OLGA: Isn't it?

IRINA: Horrible.

OLGA: Always the fool he is.

MASHA (*sings*): An oak of green
                In Lokomoryeh
                A chain of gold
                Upon the oak
                A chain of gold
                Upon the oak—
                . . . A chain of gold
                . . . upon the oak.

OLGA: You out of sorts today? (MASHA *hums, puts on her hat.*) Are you out of sorts today? Where are you going?

MASHA: Home.

IRINA: . . . You're going *home* . . . ?

TUZENBACH: You're leaving a *birthday* . . . ?

MASHA: All the same to me. I'll be back this evening. (*Kisses* IRINA.) Again, always, be healthy, be happy. In the old days. When Father was alive—we would have half the garrison come to our birthdays—didn't we? And what a lot of commotion. But what do we have today, a person and a half and it is dead as the bottom of the sea. Me, yes, I'll go—I'm down today—I'm so out of sorts and not cheerful, so pay me no attention—it's alright. We'll talk later my darling—now goodbye. I think I'd better go.

IRINA: You are so . . .

OLGA: No, I understand you, Masha.

SOLYONY: If a man, if a man *philosophizes,* then it is, it is, it is *philosophizing*—or we can say that it is "sophistry"—but if a *woman*, if a *woman* should take to *philosophizing*, then it is, it is a case of "tap me on the head."

MASHA (*pause*): What *can* that mean? What *can* that mean, you horrid man . . . ? What did you mean by that?

SOLYONY: Nothing.

MASHA: You didn't?

SOLYONY: "Hardly had he cried 'alack'
Before the bear was on his back . . ."

MASHA (*to* OLGA): Do you think you might stop crying?

(*Enter* ANFISA *and* FERAPONT *with a cake.*)

ANFISA: Come in, come in, little father—are your feet clean? Yes. Here—from the District Board, from Mikhail Ivanych Protopopov—a . . . a "pie."

IRINA: Thank you. Do thank him for me.

FERAPONT: What?

IRINA: THANK HIM.

OLGA: Nanny, dear—give him some pie.

FERAPONT: What?

IRINA: *THANK HIM!!!!!*

OLGA: Will you give him some pie? Ferapont, please, go along, you'll get your pie in there.

FERAPONT: What?

ANFISA: Come along, little one, come along now. (*Exits.*)

MASHA: I don't like Protopopov—Mikhail Potapych or *Ivanych* or whatever he is. I don't like him. Who invited him?

IRINA: I didn't invite him.

MASHA: Well, *fine* . . .

(*Enter* CHEBUTYKIN, *followed by a soldier with a silver samovar—murmur of astonishment.*)

OLGA (*exiting*): A *samovar*—oh, God . . . oh, no . . .

IRINA: Ivan Romanych, my dove, what is it you're doing?

TUZENBACH: I told you.

MASHA: Ivan Romanych, no, you have no shame . . .

CHEBUTYKIN: My dearest ones, my good, my only ones . . . those that are to me the dearest objects in the world. I am a lonely, worthless man, an old man, soon I will be sixty—there is nothing of the good in me except my love for you. If it were not for you, I would have left off living many years ago. (*To* IRINA:) My darling child—I've known you since the day that you were born. I bore you in my arms, I loved your sainted mother . . .

IRINA: Yes. But why such lavish presents?

CHEBUTYKIN: Lavish presents . . . lavish presents . . . *Damn* it, then, take, take that samovar away. "Such lavishness . . ." (*To orderly:*) Put it in there . . .

ANFISA (*passing through the parlor*): My dears—An "unknown colonel"—got his topcoat off already—coming in here, come to call—Arinushka, now, you be sweet—you mind, now—oh, Lord, and we need breakfast, too . . .

TUZENBACH: Vershinin, I would think . . .

VERSHININ (*entering, to* MASHA *and* IRINA): I have the honor to present myself: Vershinin—I am so very glad to be here with you—oh, Lord, *look* at you . . .

IRINA: Sit down, please. We're so glad to have you.

VERSHININ: And I, how glad am I to be here, can you know? I don't think you can know. Yes. Three girls. There are three of you. And, looking back, no, I can't see the faces, but I remember—so strongly—Colonel Prozoroff and his three little girls . . . (*Pause.*) How time passes. Oh, Lord, the ways in which time . . . (*Pause.*)

TUZENBACH: Alexandr Ignatyevich is from Moscow.

IRINA: You are from Moscow, you're from Moscow?

VERSHININ: Yes. I am. Your late father, when he commanded Moscow battery I was an officer in his brigade. (*To* MASHA:) Yes. Now I begin to remember you. Yes, I do.

MASHA: I don't remember you.

IRINA: Olga. Olga. Ol . . . will you come in here . . . ?

(OLGA *enters.*)

IRINA: It seems Lieutenant Colonel Vershinin is from *Moscow.*

VERSHININ: And you must be Olga Sergeyevna—"the oldest daughter." And you, you must be *Maria,* and you are the youngest, and you are *Irina.* Isn't that it?

OLGA: You're from Moscow?

VERSHININ: Many years. Studied there, entered the service. Served in Moscow many years. Finally received my command here, transferred here—as you see—but, you know, it is so *vague,* really, so vague—only I remember, there were *three* of you. Just an impression, really, while your father, when I close my eyes—I have

him right before me. In my memory, as if he were alive.
I used to call on you.

OLGA: . . . you.

VERSHININ: Alexandr Ignatyevich.

OLGA: Alexandr Ignatyevich.

VERSHININ: Yes.

OLGA: I *remarked* it, because we're returning there . . .

IRINA: We're moving back to Moscow—our plan is to be
installed by autumn—back on . . .

OLGA: . . . yes.

IRINA: Old Basmannaya Street.

OLGA: "Back on the old street . . ."

(*The two girls laugh.*)

MASHA: And out of the blue. We meet a fellow townsman.
Oh. Wait, wait, wait. Olga—Olga. They said, at our
house, they used to say "the lovesick major . . ." You
were . . .

VERSHININ: Yes.

MASHA: But you were still a lieutenant—but they called
you "the lovesick major." You were stuck on some . . .
some . . .

VERSHININ: "The lovesick major . . ."

MASHA: But you had a moustache. (*Pause.*) How old you've
grown. Oh, my Lord . . .

VERSHININ: Well. You see. When I was "the lovesick major"
I was young. I was young. And in love.

MASHA: . . . yes.

VERSHININ: And I . . . it's not the same now, you see.

OLGA: But, you haven't gone gray—do you know? You're "old," but you're *not* old . . .

VERSHININ: Well, that is it then.

OLGA: You're somehow . . .

VERSHININ: I'm forty-three. How long since you left Moscow?

OLGA: Eleven years. Oh—Masha, Masha. Stop it now, stop it now, or I'll start in too . . . (*Crying.*)

MASHA: No, I'm fine—and you lived on what street?

VERSHININ: Old Basmannaya.

OLGA: So did we . . .

VERSHININ: At one time I'd lived on Nemetskaya Street. And from there I could walk down to the barracks. I used to *walk* it . . . there is this bridge on the way . . . the water roars beneath it. Every day, I'd take that walk . . . I'd take that walk and something in the lonely place . . . or in *me*, you see, would, would grow quite sad. (*Pause.*) While here—a broad, open, a *lovely* river.

OLGA: Well, except it's vicious cold, and the *mosquitos* . . .

VERSHININ: *Oh* no, *oh* no. A good and a healthy Slavic climate. The *forest*, the *river*, the *birches* you have! Which, to me, are, in their modest selves, most beautiful trees. How blessed you are to live here. In this magnificent country, and why, I'm puzzled by it, though, is the railway depot forty miles off. Why is that? No one can tell me why that is so.

SOLYONY: Why is that?

VERSHININ: Yes.

SOLYONY: In fact, because, *because, had it been nearer* . . . (*Pause.*) It would *not* have been forty miles off. (*Pause.*)

TUZENBACH: And they say wit has disappeared.

OLGA: No, no. I remember you!

VERSHININ: I knew your sainted mother.

CHEBUTYKIN: . . . Kingdom of Heaven unto her . . .

IRINA: She is buried in Moscow.

OLGA: At the Nova-Devichyeh.

MASHA: And I'm beginning to forget her face. Already. Could you have imagined that? In the same way that we will be forgotten.

VERSHININ: Yes. They'll forget us.

MASHA: Will they not?

VERSHININ: Yes. Which is the nature of the world. And that is our *fate* and there's nothing to be done. And that which seems to us now so significant, so "important," a time will come . . . it will certainly come, when it will be forgotten. (*Pause.*) And do you know, I believe, I find it quite interesting, I do, *that we cannot know* that we have *no* way of foretelling what *specifically* will be seen as important and what as, as pitiful and comic. *Copernicus*, let us say. Christopher Columbus—did not their work and lives, at first, seem laughable, misguided, and beneath contempt? While the works of those long forgotten were held to be universal truth? I think so. And it so could happen, could it not, that our present life, of which we think so well, to which we are so reconciled, will come, in time, to be seen as *unwise*, uncomfortable, strange. *Unclean* perhaps, perhaps even sinful.

TUZENBACH: Well, we don't know. *Do* we? Neither do we know that our life will not be called elevated. And thought of with great respect—you see—we have no . . . *tortures, executions,* no . . . *invasions* . . .

VERSHININ: And yet.

TUZENBACH: Yes, and yet, yes. How much suffering . . .

SOLYONY: Kitty, kitty, kitty, kitty, eat your vittles and philosophize a bit . . .

TUZENBACH: Vassily Vassilych. I require you, with all courtesy, to please leave me alone. You understand me?

SOLYONY: Kitty, kitty, kitty.

TUZENBACH: Yes. How tedious. (*To* VERSHININ:) However.

VERSHININ: Yes.

TUZENBACH: However.

VERSHININ: Yes.

TUZENBACH: That suffering which we observe.

VERSHININ: Yes.

TUZENBACH: And there is so much of it.

VERSHININ: There is.

TUZENBACH: Is it not possible.

VERSHININ: Yes.

TUZENBACH: That it's *nature*.

VERSHININ: That's to say the nature of the suffering today.

TUZENBACH: Yes. Does it not speak to the possibility of a, an *uplift* in the moral tenor of the times? Don't you *think*?

VERSHININ: Yes. I do.

CHEBUTYKIN: You have said, Baron, that our life today might be called *elevated*. How is it, then, that, all the same, the people are short. (*Stands.*) *I'm* short . . . look how short I am. Then I must thank you, you see, for your holding out to me this consolation . . .

(*Violin plays offstage.*)

MASHA: Our brother Andrei.

IRINA: Our scholar. Picked out to be a professor. Papa was a military man . . .

MASHA: Yes.

IRINA: But his son has chosen differently.

MASHA: Though in accord with Papa's wishes.

IRINA: Yes.

OLGA: Well, and it's his turn to bear a little teasing these days, for it seems he has fallen slightly in love.

IRINA: A certain local miss.

OLGA: Yes.

IRINA: Who will be with us today, in all possibility.

MASHA: You know. She dresses herself—she dresses herself as if she were a pig. It's not that it's ugly. It's just, it's pathetic. Little yellow "skirts," you know, with "fringe," this "fringelike" affair, and that *trim red blouse*. Her cheeks glowing. So "scrubbed." I . . . don't *say* that

Andrei's in love with her. No, say he may be diverting himself. But don't say that our brother has no taste. *Additionally,* I heard that she is marrying Protopopov, of the District Board. Joy to their union. Andrei—Andrei . . . come here, dearest. My brother, Andrei Sergeyevich.

VERSHININ: Vershinin.

ANDREI: Prozoroff. Delighted. You're posted here as battery commander.

VERSHININ: I am.

ANDREI: I congratulate you.

OLGA: Come from Moscow.

ANDREI: And that is a pity. As now my good sisters will give you no peace.

VERSHININ: We've already had time to let them tire of me.

IRINA: Look at this magnificent little frame—Andrei gave it to me. He gave it to me today, and he made it himself. (*Pause.*)

VERSHININ: I . . . yes, a, a frame.

IRINA: And that sweet little one above the piano, he made that one too.

OLGA: Here is what he is. Our boy. A *scholar,* a *master* of the *violin,* an *artificer* of all sorts of . . . in short, a jack-of-all-trades, Andrei, don't go, and always, and this is your manner too, you're always walking away. Come here . . .

MASHA: Come here, come on, then.

ANDREI: Please. Leave me alone. Please.

MASHA: And now we've angered you. Oh . . . You're so *sensitive!* You are. Alexandr Ignatyevich here, used to be called a *lovesick* major, and did he take on about it? No.

VERSHININ: No.

MASHA: And you. We'll call you, the demon um um um, the demon lover, no, the lovestruck fiddler, no . . .

IRINA: The puppy-love professor.

MASHA: No, the . . .

IRINA: He's in love. Andrei's in love . . .

CHEBUTYKIN: "For this alone has Nature placed us in the world—for *love!*"

ANDREI: Alright. Fine. Thank you.

CHEBUTYKIN: "Just for love . . ."

ANDREI: Thank you. Enough. Alright. Oh, Lord. I am so tired. I am not quite myself, as they say. Up until four reading. Shut my eyes. Couldn't sleep. Everything racing through my mind. Then there's the early sun and the bedroom's bursting with light. You know, this summer I think that while I'm here I'm going to translate this one book from the English.

VERSHININ: You read English?

ANDREI: Our *father,* his spirit rest in peace, saddled us with an education. *Since his death (pause)* since his death, I've noticed, and they must be connected, that I've put on weight. I've gained all of this weight. In the past year. As if I had been, as if my body had been freed from fetters. Yes. We all speak French, German, and English. My sisters and I, Irina knowing some Italian, too, into the bargain. (*Pause.*) And what a price we paid.

MASHA: To speak three languages in this town is not an accomplishment. It is a deformity.

VERSHININ: Well, *no*.

MASHA: Yes.

VERSHININ: *Really* . . .

MASHA: Yes.

VERSHININ: How can that be. How can there be a town so dull but that it cannot be enlivened by intelligence?

MASHA: Look around you.

VERSHININ: No, truly . . . say there are one hundred thousand people. A town of a hundred thousand backward, coarse, uneducated. And there, in the midst of that town, three such as yourselves. Now. *As you live your lives*—it goes without saying that you will not overcome the mass. The gray mass which surrounds you—you will be subsumed. For this is how life works. *But* you shall not be without influence—to the contrary. Your influence *will, will* imperceptibly but certainly make itself felt. And *after* you, perhaps, another three, like yourselves, another three, six, twelve more, each, you see, adding their influence—over time—such that, over time, you will be the majority. In two, three hundred years. Such that life on earth will have become unutterably beautiful. Men need such a life. We do not have it, but we dream of it. We anticipate it. We wait. We wonder. We prepare for it. For the need to know. More than our ancestors—more than those who've gone before . . . more than they know . . . hah hah . . . hah . . . and you say that *you* are mired in redundancy.

MASHA (*taking off her hat*): I'm going to stay for breakfast.

IRINA: You know. I wish that someone had been here to *write that down.*

TUZENBACH: You say that after many years life on earth will become beautiful. Yes. I think so. But in order to *partake*, if I may say, to partake now of that beauty, to "participate" in it now, though it be from afar, we must *plan* for it, we must *work* for it. We must . . .

VERSHININ: Yes, yes. Well, I *think* so. What a *raft* of flowers you have here. Your home is so beautiful. All my life I have been banging about small, dingy flats with the two chairs, the couch, the samovar and the same smoking stove, all of my life. I have lacked *precisely* these flowers. *Oh*, well, then; *oh* well . . . *oh* my . . .

TUZENBACH: Yes. One must work. I know, you're thinking "Yes. A sentimental German." On my mother's grave, I am a *Russian*. My *name's* German, I am a Russian, I don't even *speak* German. My father's Russian *Orthodox*, and *he* even, you see, is not fluent in German.

VERSHININ: I have thought. I have often thought what if we could begin our lives anew. If we could *remember* the life we've lived and use that as a draft, as a rough draft, if you will. Do you see. Learning from our mistakes— arranging *everything*, as we know its result, you see; to *please*, to *complement*, as one would decorate a house, or this apartment, with *flowers*. And light—with a sense of the whole. My wife is unwell. I have two small girls. If I were to start again, if I were to, I would not marry, no, I'd . . .

(*Enter* KULYGIN.)

KULYGIN (*to* IRINA): Dear sister. May I congratulate you. Upon your name day. May I *wish* you, with all that at my command. *Health,* happiness, and all the customary wishes one addresses to a lady of your years. Then let me offer you this little "pamphlet." I wrote it. It is the history of the last fifty years of our academy. A little "tract"; scribbled from want of other idleness. But, but, but read it, do. Ladies and gentlemen. (*To* VERSHININ:) Kulygin—instructor at our academy and civil counselor. (*To* IRINA:) *In* this book you will find a roster of all those having completed our course in the last half century. That you will find in here. *Feci quod potui, faciant meliora potentes.* I hope my book amuses you. (*Kisses* MASHA.)

IRINA (*of book*): You gave me one at Easter.

KULYGIN: Ha. Well. Then I suppose you have superfluity. Dear *Colonel,* if you will permit me. (*Gives him the book.*) And, perhaps someday, in an hour of boredom, my poor book . . .

VERSHININ: Thank you. I thank you very much. I am so glad to've met you . . .

OLGA: Are you going? *No* . . .

IRINA: No, no, stay, please. For breakfast, at least—please.

OLGA: Please—oblige us.

VERSHININ: Well. (*Pause.*) It seems I have found myself involved in a *birthday* . . . (*pause*) . . . a birthday.

OLGA (*inviting him into the next room*): Come with me.

VERSHININ: Yes. I will . . . (*Exiting.*) Congratulations . . . (*Exits.*)

KULYGIN: Today, ladies and gentlemen, is Sunday. Sunday is a day of rest. Let us rest, therefore, and each, in that way appropriate to his age and rank, rejoice and make merry. We'll take the carpets up and store them away til the winter comes—with Persian powder or with naphthalene—*Romans* enjoyed health because they knew this rule: *mens sana in corpore sano,* they understood both *work* and *rest.* And, so, their lives *flowed,* along certain prescribed *forms.* Our headmaster has said that the chief thing in a life is form. That which loses its form ends. But that which *possesses* it, do you see? And in our daily lives it is the same. Masha, my wife, loves me. My wife loves me. The *window* curtains, which, just as the carpets . . . must . . . Today I have a high heart! Masha—a cheerful heart. At four o'clock we're to be at the headmaster's. Who has arranged the outing for the faculty families.

MASHA: No, I'm not . . . No. I'm not going. (*Pause.*)

KULYGIN: . . . Darling.

MASHA: No.

KULYGIN: My darling. Why?

MASHA: No. I, uh. Fine. I'll tell you later. No. I'll go. Alright. I'll go. Alright? I'll go. If you'll not PLAGUE me . . . will you. Please . . . ? (*Walks away.*)

KULYGIN: . . . and, afterwards . . . we'll spend the evening at the headmaster's. Who does, who is so social. Despite it all. Isn't he? An excellent man. I think. A good soul. An excellent man. At the conference yesterday, he says, he says, "Tired, Fyodor Ilych . . . *tired.*" (*Pause.*) "Tired . . ." (*Looks at the clock on the wall, then at his watch.*) Your clock is seven minutes fast. "Yes . . ." he says . . . "tired . . ."

(*A violin plays offstage.*)

OLGA (*reemerging*): Gentlemen. If you please. Be so good as to be seated. Your breakfast. A pie.

KULYGIN: Oh. Olga, my dear Olga. *Olga.* Yesterday I worked from morning til eleven o'clock at night. And, yes, I was fatigued—yes, I was. But today, I feel happy . . . my dear. (*Exits.*)

CHEBUTYKIN: . . . a *pie.*

OLGA: Yes.

CHEBUTYKIN: Magnificent.

MASHA: But no drinking. No drinking today. Do you hear me? It's no good for you to drink.

CHEBUTYKIN: Please. I'm over it. Would you please? For the last two years. My little mother. Two years. What's it going to hurt?

MASHA: No drinking. Don't you *dare* to do it. And, oh God, protect me. The whole evening. Bored to madness by the headmaster.

TUZENBACH: Don't go.

MASHA: Mmm.

TUZENBACH: In your place I wouldn't.

CHEBUTYKIN: Don't you go. My pumpkin.

MASHA: Fine. "Don't go." The cursed life of one of the damned. (*Exits to reception room.*)

CHEBUTYKIN: Now, *Masha* . . . (*Also exits.*)

SOLYONY (*going into the reception room*): Cluck, cluck, cluck, cluck.

TUZENBACH: Fine, Vassily Vassilych. That will do.

KULYGIN (*reentering*): To your health, Colonel. Yes. I'm an academic . . . yes. I am "one of our own" here. Masha's husband. Here at the house. One of "les nôtres." What a woman. So kind.

VERSHININ: Some of the pepper vodka. (*To* OLGA:) Your health. Yes. I feel so good here.

(*Only* IRINA *and* TUZENBACH *remain in the parlor.*)

IRINA: Masha's out of sorts today.

TUZENBACH: Mmm.

IRINA: At eighteen she married one who seemed to her the most intelligent of men. Now . . .

TUZENBACH: Yes?

IRINA: . . . he is a *kind* man. He may be the kindest of men—but he's not the most intelligent.

OLGA (*offstage*): On, Andrei . . . do come, finally . . .

ANDREI (*offstage*): . . . I'm coming.

TUZENBACH: What are you thinking about?

IRINA: I am thinking . . . I do not like your Solyony. I don't like him, and I'm frightened of him. All that he says are stupid things.

TUZENBACH: Yes. He's strange.

IRINA (*to herself*): . . . strange . . .

TUZENBACH: I'm sorry for him. He annoys me, too. But I pity him.

IRINA: Do you?

TUZENBACH: Yes. I think he's shy. When we're alone he can be quite . . . engaging . . . quite intelligent. Tender, even, perhaps. In company he is crude, as you say, and coarse. No. Don't go. (*Pause.*) Let them go in. We'll join them in a while. Let me be near you for a moment yet. And tell me. What you're thinking of. (*Pause.*) And here you are. Twenty years old. And I am not yet thirty. How many days lie before us? (*Pause.*) A procession of days. Full of love. Full of my love for you.

IRINA: Nikolai Lvovich . . .

TUZENBACH: . . . my feeling is that *love* . . . that *struggle*, that a thirst for *labor*—why can we not say "a thirst" . . . ? . . . all the things in life . . . have merged with my love for you. Oh—with my love for you—and your *beauty.* And life seems so beautiful—what . . . ?

IRINA: I'm thinking of what you're saying.

TUZENBACH: . . . yes . . . ?

IRINA: You say that "life is beautiful." Yes. It seems so to you. But for my sisters. And for me. It has not yet been so. We . . . (*Pause.*) Do you know what it is to be *cloyed*? To become *jaded*? To live as it . . . oh, now I'm crying— what does *that* accomplish? (*Pause.*) Work. "Work" . . . you see . . . ? Through *work* . . . it's through work that one can find happiness. And if one does *not* work . . . and that's why we are unhappy. *Isn't* it? Because we have nothing to do. We are born of people who despise work.

(*Enter* NATALYA IVANOVNA.)

NATALYA: Yes. They're at breakfast. And I'm late. (*Looks at herself in the mirror. To herself:*) My hair. Is. Good.

Enough. (*To* IRINA:) Dearest Irina Sergeyevna. My congratulations. (*Kisses her.*) Here is a kiss . . . and what a slew of guests we have. They'll make me self-conscious . . . so many of them. I swear that they will. *Baron* . . .

OLGA (*entering*): . . . at last . . .

NATALYA: Congratulations on your *birthday* girl . . . on your . . . "*birthday*" girl . . . but, do you know, you just have so much "company" . . .

OLGA: . . . we . . .

NATALYA: . . . it makes people "*shy*" . . .

OLGA: . . . it's only the old . . . Oh, Lord.

NATALYA: What?

OLGA: No.

NATALYA: What?

OLGA: Your belt.

NATALYA: What?

OLGA: You're wearing a green belt.

NATALYA: . . . yes.

OLGA: . . . that.

NATALYA: That isn't good?

OLGA (*pause*): No.

NATALYA: Is it "bad luck"?

OLGA: Is it bad luck? Is it "bad luck . . . ?" Noo . . .

NATALYA: Then . . . ? (*Pause.*) *What?* It doesn't "go" . . .

OLGA: No, it . . .

NATALYA: What?

OLGA: It looks *strange*.

NATALYA: It looks strange. Why? (*Pause*.) Why? The "color."

OLGA: Yes.

NATALYA: Because it's *green* . . .

OLGA: Because . . .

NATALYA: It isn't "green" you know.

OLGA: It isn't? (*They exit to reception room*.)

NATALYA: No.

OLGA: What *is* it?

NATALYA: What is it? *Gray* . . . *Putty*, sort of . . .

OLGA: It's "*gray*"?

KULYGIN: And you, Irina. To you, a fine fiancé, and a healthy marriage. The time for which, I think I may say, is . . .

CHEBUTYKIN: Natalya Ivanovna, to you, too, I wish such a fiancé.

KULYGIN: Natalya Ivanovna already possesses such a . . .

MASHA: Well. I'll *take* a wee dram, then. Yes. I will. A life of knock-down jollity and ease, and God damn me to hell if it isn't so.

KULYGIN: *Zéro pour conduite*.

VERSHININ (*of liquor*): This is delicious. And it's made of what?

SOLYONY: Bat's blood.

VERSHININ: . . . it's . . . ?

IRINA: Oh, God. *Must* we?

OLGA: For supper we have: roast turkey. Sweet potato pie. With apples . . . thank God that I have the time . . . *DO* come this evening. Everyone.

VERSHININ: May I come too?

IRINA: Please.

NATALYA: Yes. We do things simply here.

CHEBUTYKIN: "For love it is that for which a loving God has put us in the world . . ."

ANDREI: Isn't it "cloying"? Don't you think?

(FEDOTIK *and* RODE *enter with flowers.*)

FEDOTIK: . . . breakfast *already* is it . . . ?

RODE: Yes. Breakfast. Yes. Breakfast.

FEDOTIK: One moment. (*Takes a snapshot.*) One more . . . hold that please . . . One . . . *Two* . . . (*Takes a snapshot.*)

RODE: CONGRATULATIONS. What do I *not* wish you? What a day! May you have it *all*. Everything! This morning. I was out. On a walk. With the *academy* boys, you know?

FEDOTIK: And now you may move.

RODE: You may know, I teach gymnastics there.

FEDOTIK: Irina Sergeyevna: you may move now. (*Pause.*) How attractive you are today. Here, by the way, is a "top" . . . I want you to hear the sound that it makes.

IRINA: Oh, yes. (*To all, of the top:*) You *hear* this . . . ?

MASHA: "An oak of green, in Lokomoryeh. A chain of gold *upon* the oak . . ." A golden chain upon it. What in the *world* would you think I am saying that for? That phrase. Did this ever happen to you? Been inside my head since *morning*, it's been stuck to me.

KULYGIN: Thirteen at table . . . ?

RODE: But can it be we attach weight to superstition?

KULYGIN: "Thirteen at table, then two of the thirteen are in Love." And could one of that two, God save the mark, be *you* . . . Ivan Romanych . . . ? Be *you*!!!?

CHEBUTYKIN: I am an old sinner. Why, however, why Natalya Ivanovna should be blushing *eludes* me . . .

(NATALYA *runs out of the room.* ANDREI *follows.*)

ANDREI: Oh, please . . . No, no. It's not important. Please.

NATALYA: No. They make me feel . . . I'm sorry. I feel so *ashamed* . . . and, and, and . . . now I've left the *table*! Oh, Lord. I'm sorry. I can't . . . I can't . . . (*Covers her face with her hand.*)

ANDREI: My dearest. Please. Please. You don't have to *upset* yourself . . . they're . . . *please*. They're *joking*. They're speaking out of *love* for you. They *are*. My *darling* . . . my good one . . . What are they but kind, warmhearted people? *Nothing*. They love me, and they love you. Yes. Come here. Come here . . . they can't see us . . .

NATALYA: I, I, I, I don't know how to, to . . .

ANDREI: . . . what?

NATALYA: To "comport" myself. In company.

ANDREI: Oh, no. Oh. My darling young one. Believe me. I feel so . . . I am so full of love for you . . . no, they can't see us. No, they can't. Oh, go, who led to, to you . . . ! What a mystery. I love you. I love you. Marry me. Be my wife. I love you as no one ever . . . listen to me, as no man . . . (*He kisses her. Two workmen enter and watch them kissing.*)

Act II

The same set as Act One.

Eight o'clock in the evening. Offstage, on the street, the sound of an accordion playing. Enter NATALYA *in a dressing gown, carrying a candle into the dark room. She stops at the door leading to Andrei's room.*

NATALYA: Andriushka . . . ? Andriushka . . . ? Are you? Are you reading? . . . are you awake . . . ?

(*She goes to an adjacent door, opens it.* ANDREI *comes out of her room and sees her looking in at the other door.*)

I was just checking the fire is out. You know . . . *Shrovetide*, and the servants are . . . do you think I'm foolish?

ANDREI: Natalya . . .

NATALYA: To be "concerned." Do you think it's silly of me? But yesterday evening. *Midnight*, I was walking through the dining room, and there was a candle burning. On the tablecloth. I *worry* . . . and I . . . who *lit* it,

31

who left it *burning* . . . (*Puts her candle down.*) What, what time is it?

ANDREI (*looks at the clock*): Past eight. Quarter past eight.

NATALYA: A quarter past eight . . . Irina isn't back . . .

ANDREI: No.

NATALYA: Irina is not back. Olga isn't back. No. Oh. Lord. They work so hard. They're at the *teacher's* meeting . . . Irina is at the *telegraph* . . . this morning I said to her "*Darling* . . ." I said to your sister . . . "Take *care* of yourself . . . Irina. My *jewel* . . ." And did she listen? . . . a quarter past eight . . .

ANDREI: Yes.

NATALYA: I am afraid our Bobik isn't well. Why is he cold? Why is he so cold? Yesterday he's burning, and today he's cold. I'm frightened, I . . .

ANDREI: It's nothing, Natalya . . .

NATALYA: It *is* . . .

ANDREI: The boy is healthy.

NATALYA: *Is* he? (*Pause.*) In *any* case. The *diet*. Let him *eat* it, you see. I'm, I'm so afraid for him. The mummers are coming at nine. I wish they weren't. Andrei . . . ?

ANDREI: . . . but we invited them.

NATALYA: This morning. My angel. Woke up and looked at me, he *looked* at me, and . . . "*smiled*." And I saw such *recognition*. In that smile. He . . .

ANDREI: . . . he "knew" you.

NATALYA: And, yes, and "*Bobik*," I said. "*Morning*, darling!" And he *laughed*. You know. What *don't* they understand? They understand it all. I think. I think they do. So, I'll, Andriushka, I'll have them send the mummers away when they come.

ANDREI: But . . .

NATALYA: Yes?

ANDREI: You see?

NATALYA: Yes?

ANDREI: My *sisters* . . . they've . . . they've *sent* for them . . .

NATALYA: . . . I'll . . .

ANDREI: . . . n'as it is their *house* . . .

NATALYA: No, no, no, I'll tell them too. I'll tell them what I did. They're so kind. *Aren't* they? I find them exceptional. (*Exiting.*) For supper I've told them to lay out some yoghurt . . .

   (ANDREI *starts to interject.*)

Doctor says . . . *yes,* I know, but if you don't *eat* it, how are you going to lose the weight? No. He's cold. Bobik is cold in that room. It's the *room,* and we must find him another one til it turns warm. *Irina's* room! It's *perfect* for a child. It's *dry,* it's *sunny,* and why couldn't she move in with Olga for a while? You know? She's never here during the day. Isn't that true? Andriushka. You're so quiet.

ANDREI: . . . just thinking.

NATALYA: And there was something I wanted to tell you. Oh. Oh yes. Ferapont. From the District Board. Is here for you.

ANDREI: Alright.

NATALYA: Send him in?

ANDREI: Yes. (*She exits.* FERAPONT *enters.*) "Captain of my Soul." How are we?

FERAPONT: The chairman has sent down some papers.

ANDREI: *Has* he.

FERAPONT: And this book. (*Hands them to* ANDREI.)

ANDREI: Uh huh. And what brings you here so dis-punctually.

FERAPONT (*pause*): What?

ANDREI: Why are you here so late?

FERAPONT: . . . I'm late . . . ?

ANDREI: It's past *eight.*

FERAPONT: Yes, sir. It is. Sir. When I arrived here, it was *light.* They kept putting me off. "The master's *busy* . . ." "Oh. Well. If he's '*busy*' . . . then, you know, I'll, I'll, I'll . . . *wait.*" I'm sorry . . . ?

ANDREI: What? What? Nothing. Never mind. Tomorrow we're off in the morning. But I'll stop in. Things to do. *Don't* we? So good to have an "occupation."

FERAPONT: Sir?

ANDREI: Good to have somewhere to *go. Isn't* it? (*Pause.*) Old one. (*Pause.*) Eh? Our *life.* And I say: "Go under-stand it." "*Explain*" it to me. When I can take up a *book* . . . out of *boredom*, at *random*, and my hand falls upon, my old, my *university* lectures. Isn't that "odd," then? I think so. Who is it that thinks so? The secretary of the District Board, of which board Protopopov sits as chair-man, while I revel in the honor of working as secretary *to* that board, and while the highest honor to which I might in my delusion aspire is to be nominated to sit with those dignitaries. I fall asleep each night fantasizing that I am a Russian *Treasure*, you see, a renowned light of the university whose name is synonymous with *learning, courage, insight* . . .

FERAPONT: What?

ANDREI: Well. If you could *hear,* would I be *talking* to you . . . ? (*Pause.*) I need somebody to talk to. My *wife* doesn't understand. If I talked to my *sisters* they'd laugh me to scorn. I think they would. Who's going to listen to me? I don't care for *clubs* . . . but I would sit with *joy,* I would, at *Tyestov's,* or Slavyansky *Bazaar,* yes, I would. At any Moscow . . .

FERAPONT: A contractor was telling me that in Moscow, the other day, some men were eating *blinis,* and one man ate forty blinis. And died, is what he said. (*Pause.*) . . . Thirty or forty.

ANDREI: . . . there you are. (*Pause.*) In the grand dining room. Of a great Moscow restaurant. You know no one. And no one knows you. At The Same Time, you understand, there is a feeling of *belonging.* Yes. I use that word. Here, everyone knows everyone. And to what end, for we're all strangers. And so lonely. So . . .

FERAPONT: What? (*Pause.*) And the same man was saying—well, he might be lying, who's to say? That they have stretched a *hawser* crost the whole of Moscow. (*Pause.*)

ANDREI: What for?

FERAPONT: What?

ANDREI: For what purpose?

FERAPONT: I do not have the honor to know. And the man was saying.

ANDREI: What a load of garbage. Have you *been* to Moscow?

FERAPONT: Can't say that I have. For it did not fit with God's Will to guide me there. (*Pause.*) May I go now?

ANDREI: Well, yes. You may. God bless you. Come back tomorrow for the papers. Will you. Now go along. Goodbye.

(FERAPONT *exits.*)

Yes. To "work" at a thing. (*Pause.*) Isn't it? (*Exits.*)

(*Enter* MASHA *and* VERSHININ. *While they go on with their discourse, a maid enters and lights candles.*)

MASHA: I don't know. (*Pause.*) I don't know. Habit is a contributory factor, I know. When we lost our orderlies, you know, when Father died, we'd come to be so used to them. No, in any case, though, perhaps not in other places, but here, in *our* town, I've always found that the most decent people were the military.

VERSHININ: Would you like some tea?

MASHA: They'll serve the tea soon. They married me off at eighteen. Frightened of my husband. In awe of him. There he was, a *teacher*. There *I* was. I'd barely finished school. He seemed so *learned*. Do you know? So *wise*, to me. And so *important*. Regrettably, those feelings have changed.

VERSHININ: . . . have changed. Yes.

MASHA: And I'm not speaking specifically, or, or I'm not speaking *exclusively* of just my husband. I'm inured to him. But I *am* speaking of the nonmilitary portion of the population, when I find them coarse, ill-bred, ill-mannered, lacking in *grace; so* many civilians, and I am *disturbed* by this behavior, which is insufficiently polite, and . . . *gracious.* And to be among his *"teachers"* is torture for me.

VERSHININ: . . . it's . . . yes.

MASHA: It's *torture.* (*Pause.*)

VERSHININ: But I would observe that, civilian *or* military . . . in this town, it's much the same.

MASHA: Is it?

VERSHININ: It's the same. I think. If you listen to the educated class—in the service or not. A man. And his life is jaded. And he has worn out his *aims* . . . and he has worn out his *horses,* you see? And, and he has worn out his *wife,* and he has *used them up,* and the Russian Man deems a life of . . . "thought" in which . . .

MASHA: . . . yes . . .

VERSHININ: . . . in which he might . . .

MASHA: . . . "recapture," yes.

VERSHININ: . . . that is right . . . *regain* his spirits . . . he deems such . . . "philosophy" "not quite the thing." . . . He has grown jaded with his wife, his *children,* with the very, the very, the food he *eats,* until it all tastes of the pan, and the pan tastes of . . .

MASHA: Well. Yes. We're out of spirits today.

VERSHININ: I am out of spirits. I've had no dinner. I've had nothing since morning. My daughter is ill, I'm sick with anger at the kind of *mother* that fate has blessed her with, this morning, *shrieking* at me, from seven o'clock this morning, until I slammed the door at nine. You let me plague you with this. I talk to *no* one about this. Only you. Don't be cross with me. I have, please, I have no one. After you. (*Pause.*) No one.

(*Sound offstage.*)

MASHA: Did you hear that? Our stove rumbled. In the chimney. Just like that. It did. Just before Father died.

VERSHININ: What is that? A superstition?

MASHA: Yes.

VERSHININ: How romantic that is. What a wonderful woman you are. Magnificent. A wonderful . . . you are a wonderful woman. Even in the dark, here, I see your eyes. Sparkling . . .

MASHA (*moves*): There's more light over here.

VERSHININ: I love you. (*Pause.*) I love you. I love you. I love the way you move. I love your eyes. I dream about you. *Constantly.* You are the first thought and the last thought in my day.

MASHA: No, no, you've got me laughing. You know, you . . . *terrify* me. Don't . . . take it back. Someone is coming . . .

(*Enter* TUZENBACH *and* IRINA.)

TUZENBACH: I have a German name. I have a triple surname. Yes. I do. The Baron Tuzenbach-Kron-Altschauer. But am I a German? No. I am a Russian.

Russian Orthodox, like you. Nothing of the German is left in me. Patience. Patience, perhaps. Or call it "stubbornness." With which I pursue you. Each evening, as I see you home.

IRINA: . . . I'm tired . . . how tired I am.

TUZENBACH: . . . and every day. As I *will* see you home. As I *will:* come by the telegraph office. At the end of day. And see you home. How many years shall I see you home? Ten years? Twenty? How long? Til you banish me. (*Sees* MASHA *and* VERSHININ.) Oh yes. It's you. Home at last.

IRINA: Thank God I'm home. (*Pause.*) Woman comes in. She wants to telegraph her brother in Saratov. That her son has died. (*Pause.*) Can't remember the address. She sends it just like that: "Saratov." She's *crying* . . . I was so *rude* to her . . . "I haven't the *time*, you see?" Oh, Lord. It all comes out wrong. (*Pause. Sighs.*) We're having the mummers this evening.

MASHA: Yes.

IRINA (*sighs*): Oh *God*, I'm tired.

TUZENBACH: Back from your post.

IRINA: . . . yes.

TUZENBACH: Such a young, Unhappy Little Thing.

IRINA: I hate that office.

MASHA: You're losing weight?

IRINA: Am I?

MASHA: And, yes, you are, your face has lost its softness. You look like a young boy.

TUZENBACH: No, that's the hairstyle.

: I'm going to have to find a new position.

ʌHA: . . . are you?

IRINA: Yes. It is *toil*, you see, without poetry. Not quite what I dreamed of.

MASHA: . . . Mmm.

IRINA: . . . without *thought* . . . with . . . (*Sound of knocking.*) The doctor . . . (*To* TUZENBACH:) Knock back to him. Will you? (TUZENBACH *knocks on the floor.* IRINA *sighs.*) He'll come up now. We are going to have to do something, you know. He and Andrei went to the club and they lost again. They say Andrei lost over two hundred roubles.

MASHA: . . . Mmm.

IRINA: Two weeks *past*, he lost, in *December* he lost. I wish to God that he'd get it done and lose *everything*. Lose *everything*. Then, maybe, we'd *quit* this town. Oh, Lord. My dearest God. I dream of Moscow. Every night. It's an obsession. Just like a mad woman. Til June. I am supposed to wait til June. "We move in June." But we have *February*, we have *March*, we have . . . *April* . . . we . . . almost half a *year*. We have *May* . . .

MASHA: We have these, Natalya doesn't know he's lost.

IRINA: To her it's all the same. (*Sighs.*)

(CHEBUTYKIN *comes in, sits down. He takes out a newspaper.*)

MASHA: And here he is. Has he paid his rent?

IRINA: No. Not for eight months. No.

MASHA: Slipped his mind.

IRINA: . . . seems . . . (*They laugh.*)

MASHA: Oh. Doesn't he sit like a *Pasha*.

(*Everyone laughs. Pause.*)

IRINA: Alexandr Ignatyevich?

VERSHININ (*sighs*): Oh, *I* don't know . . . do we not have *tea*. I would give all that is in my power to *bestow* for half a glass of tea.

CHEBUTYKIN: Irina Sergeyevna . . . ?

VERSHININ: . . . haven't had a crumb since morning.

IRINA: . . . yes . . . what?

CHEBUTYKIN: "Be. So. Good . . ." Would you descend to be so good as to come here to me? *Venez ici.* (*She goes to him.*) I cannot live without you.

VERSHININ: No. No tea. Then, if we cannot have tea, may we enjoy the comforts of Philosophy.

TUZENBACH: Yes. Treating of what?

VERSHININ: Treating of . . . can we not "daydream," as it were, of what life will be in three hundred years.

TUZENBACH: Immediately. People will move in hot air balloons. *Fashions* will change. We will see the discovery and the development of the Sixth *Sense* . . .

VERSHININ: Yes.

TUZENBACH: But "life" . . .

VERSHININ: . . . "life," eyes.

TUZENBACH: *Life* will remain the same. Dark. Full of mysteries. Dark. Difficult. Unhappy. In a thousand years, too.

VERSHININ: . . . yes?

TUZENBACH: Man, man will sigh the same way and exclaim "Oh, Lord, I do not understand. It's so hard." Just as now. And free death. (*Pause.*) And yearn to live. Exactly as now. (*Pause.*)

VERSHININ: . . . but it is not, for it seems to me that it is, that *change*, and that the process of *changing*, alters every aspect of our life, little by little . . . so that, in accumulation, you see, in two or three hundred, in a thousand years—no, the date is not the point. "AT SOME TIME . . ." life will have *changed*. How can we say that it will not—as it is changing now?—into a new, a *happy* life—a life of betterment. Not that we live to *see* it, for we will not, but that now, in our suffering, in our . . . "philosophizing," in our lives *we are creating it*. And *this, this* is the purpose of our being—*this*, if you will, is our happiness. (*Pause.*)

(MASHA *laughs softly.*)

TUZENBACH: What?

MASHA: I don't know. I've been like this all day.

VERSHININ: . . . no, I have somewhat of the *groundwork* . . . but I lack your "refinement," in education, not having attended the academy. I do read. I read quite a bit, if not, perhaps, after any "system," and, so, do not, perhaps, read *what I should* . . . Meanwhile, the more I live, the more I want to know. And as I grow. Toward Death, and my hair grays, I become old, and I perceive how little, how very little I know. (*Pause.*) What do I know? One thing. It seems, and beyond contradiction: that, that, and I *ache*, you see, to demonstrate it: that there *is* no happiness. That there will *be* no happiness for us.

But that *work*, that *work* (and we *must* work) will create happiness. For our, for, for our *descendants*. Which is *not* our lot; but may belong to them.

(FEDOTIK *and* RODE *appear and strum guitars.*)

TUZENBACH: Then one ought not even to dream of happiness.

VERSHININ: No.

TUZENBACH: No. Ah—but, if I'm "happy" . . . ?

VERSHININ (*pause*): No.

TUZENBACH: . . . I'm not . . . ? Ha. Then we do not understand one another. How, then am I to convince you?

(MASHA *laughs softly.*)

Ah. Yes. *Laughter.* One million years, two million years, eighteen million years, and life will be the same. Life doesn't change. Life flows in its own ways, regardless of how we regard it. It has its own laws. With which we have no business. Or—however—which laws we can never know. (*Pause.*) Birds of passage. *Cranes*, for example; they "fly." Irrespective of what "thoughts," high or low, they may have running through their heads. They fly on. They do not know *why*, they don't know *where*; and they will fly no matter what philosopher-birds might emerge among them. Which the cranes would let philosophize as they might, while they continue to fly.

MASHA: . . . and the meaning?

TUZENBACH: The meaning? There! It's snowing! Yes. What is the meaning. (*Pause.*)

MASHA: This is the meaning: that a person must have a religion. He must seek a faith, or else his life is empty . . . it . . . it . . . to not *question*, you see? . . . why *children* are born . . . why the *cranes* fly . . . why . . . why the *stars* revolve over us . . . either one *feels* what one lives for, or else, wait a moment, or else everything is *pointless*. Do you see . . . ?

VERSHININ: But what a pity when Youth goes.

MASHA: In Gogol somewhere it says: living in the world, Ladies and Gentlemen, is Hell.

TUZENBACH: As I say. Disputing with you is *hard*. "Ladies and gentlemen."

CHEBUTYKIN (*of the newspaper*): Balzac was married. (*Pause.*) In Berdichev. (*Pause.*) I'm going to put it in my diary. (*Writes.*) Balzac . . . married . . . (*Pause.*) in Berdichev. (*Sighs.*)

IRINA (*laying out a hand of solitaire, to herself*): Balzac was married in Berdichev.

TUZENBACH: . . . the die is cast.

IRINA: . . . hmmm . . .

TUZENBACH: Maria Sergeyevna. I've sent in my papers.

MASHA: Yes. I've heard. I can't approve.

TUZENBACH: Why?

MASHA: I don't like civilians.

TUZENBACH (*sighs*): It's all the same to me. I'm not what one calls "that fine figure of a Military Man." No. Mmm. I'm not. (*Sighs.*) Well. I am going to go to work. Work. Do you work? *If only for one day.* Such that I return home and fall exhausted the *moment* I touch the bed. "Sleeping tight" . . . as workers do. (*Exits.*)

FEDOTIK (*to* IRINA): I was just on Moskovskaya Street. At Pyshivkovs. N'I picked up these colored *pencils* for you.

IRINA: No. I'm grown up.

FEDOTIK: Take them.

IRINA: You're used to seeing me and thinking of me as a *child* . . . but I've grown *up*.

FEDOTIK: . . . I got this *penknife*, too . . .

IRINA: May I see it? (FEDOTIK *hands the objects to her.*) Oh, it's *lovely* . . .

FEDOTIK: Isn't it? And I bought one for myself, too. Almost the same thing, not quite. Look: here's your major blade, and here's another blade, and here's a *third* . . .

IRINA: . . . no . . .

FEDOTIK: Yes. This is to clean your *ears* . . . a little *scissors* . . .

RODE: Doctor. How old are you?

CHEBUTYKIN: Thirty-two. (*Laughter.*)

FEDOTIK (*looking at the game of solitaire*): I'll show you another way to work it out. Gimme the cards.

(*A samovar is brought in.* ANFISA *is by the samovar. A little later* NATALYA *comes in and fusses around the table.* SOLYONY *enters and, having greeted the others, sits down at the table.*)

VERSHININ: *Lord*, what a wind!!!

MASHA: I am so sick of winter. I've quite forgotten what summer is like.

IRINA (*of cards*): It's going to come out.

MASHA: And what will that mean?

IRINA: That we will be in Moscow.

FEDOTIK: Oh. No. Your eight is on the two of spades. Won't come out. No Moscow.

CHEBUTYKIN (*of newspaper*): A raging epidemic of small-pox.

ANFISA: Masha. Now. Drink your tea up, Little One. (*To* VERSHININ:) Begging your pardon, your Honor, and your forgiveness, as I have forgotten your Patrony-mic . . .

MASHA: Bring the tea here, Nanny, if you want me to drink it.

IRINA: Nanny!

ANFISA: Yes. Nanny's coming.

NATALYA: Suckling Babies, do you know, understand *perfectly*. Did you know that? "Hello, *Bobik!*" I said, "My darling . . ." and he looked at me. In that way. And you think it's the mother in me speaking, but I assure you. I saw what I saw. *Extraordinary* child.

SOLYONY: If he were mine, I'd cut him up and boil him and eat him.

NATALYA: *Oh*, that man . . .

MASHA: Happy is he who marks not whether it is summer or winter. And it seems to me that if I were in Moscow it would be one, but *here* . . . the *weather* . . .

VERSHININ: Just the other day. Do you know? I was reading the diaries of that Frenchman who'd been convicted for the Panama fraud. He'd written his book in prison. He writes of the *bird*. He writes of the *small* things, which he saw through his window. Things he had never seen before he'd been incarcerated. All the small things. With such joy. Now, of course, that he has been set free, he'll never notice them again. Just as you, when you live in Moscow . . .

MASHA: . . . yes?

VERSHININ: Yes. When you live in Moscow, you won't see it. (*Pause.*) There *is* no happiness, and no one possesses it. All that exists is longing.

TUZENBACH (*reenters, looks at a box on the table*): But where's the candy?

IRINA: Solyony.

TUZENBACH: Ate it?

IRINA: Yes.

TUZENBACH: He ate all of it? (IRINA *nods.*)

ANFISA (*serving the tea*): A letter for you, Little Father.

VERSHININ: A letter for me? (*Takes it, reads.*) Yes. Of course. Forgive me. Maria Sergeyevna. I must go. I won't have any tea . . . (*gets up*) . . . always the same thing.

MASHA: What is it? If it's not private.

VERSHININ: The wife's poisoned herself once again. I have to go. I'll get out quietly. Oh, Lord. It's so *tawdry*. (*Pause.*) My dear woman. My dear, my sweet woman . . . forgive me. (*Exits.*)

ANFISA: And where's he off to now, and I've just served the tea . . . Yes. That man is a villain.

MASHA: Oh, *spare* him, will you please? May we have some *peace* from you?

ANFISA: *Sweetheart* . . . what . . . ? Have I *offended* you . . . ?

ANDREI (*offstage*): Anfisa . . .

ANFISA (*mimicking*): "Anfisa . . . Anfisa . . ." Calling. Calling. Sitting out there . . . (*Exits.*)

MASHA (*by the table*): Do suffer me to take a seat. Yes. Oh, well. Sprawled all over it. Your *cards*, your *tea.*

IRINA: Oh, Masha, don't scold us . . .

MASHA: Yes. Fine. I'm a scold. Don't *deal* with me. Don't *traffic* with me. Don't . . .

CHEBUTYKIN (*sitting*): "Don't deal with me, don't traffic with me . . ."

MASHA: And you, sixty years old and spewing nonsense like a child, and who the hell knows what.

NATALYA: Masha.

MASHA: *Yes.*

NATALYA: Darling Masha . . .

MASHA: *What?*

NATALYA: Why must you employ such expressions? Why? With your lovely appearance. Your . . . "carriage," you would, and I tell you frankly, be simply *enchanting*, yes, and quite appreciated in correct society. If you would only mind your speech. *Je vous prie—pardonnez-moi, Marie, mais vous avez des manières un peu grossières.*

TUZENBACH: Ha. I tell you what I need. If someone could give, if someone . . . I think we have some *cognac* here.

NATALYA: *Il paraît que mon Bobik déjà ne dort pas.* He's awake . . . my boy isn't well today, n'I must go to him. You'll all excuse me . . . ? (*Exits.*)

IRINA: Where is Alexandr Ignatyevich?

MASHA: Gone home.

IRINA: Has he?

MASHA: Something "unusual" about the wife again.

TUZENBACH (*to* SOLYONY): Always alone. Sitting. Sitting, thinking. *What* are you thinking about? Well. Let's make up. Will you? Have a drink with me. Today I am going to play the piano all night. I will play all *sorts* of rubbish. *Yes, I will.*

SOLYONY: So why do you say "make up"? Have we been quarreling?

TUZENBACH: You know. Yes. You always, *you* know what I mean. You seem to have the feeling—you know that you do, that something has "occurred." Isn't that so? Isn't it? You're a strange man. And you must admit it.

SOLYONY (*declaiming*): Yes. I am strange.
> But are we all not strange
> If one were, for the briefest nonce,
> To peek behind this drape of Normalcy, Good Don Alekko . . .

TUZENBACH: And what has Don Alekko got to do with it?

SOLYONY: When I'm with someone face to face, I'm fine. With two people . . . I'm fine. In company, however, I'm a fool. It's as simple as that. I'm glum and shy and spew all *sorts* of idiocy, *and for all that,* are you listening, I'm content that I am more *honest,* and more *noble* than many, and than *very* many, and I can establish it.

TUZENBACH: . . . I'm angry with you all the time.

SOLYONY: . . . all of the time?

TUZENBACH: Well, yes, I think you pick on me. When we're in company. You pick on me, and yet, and yet, you *do*. You mistreat me, and yet I'm drawn to you. Why is that? Why is that?

SOLYONY: . . . well . . .

TUZENBACH: I'm going to get drunk. Drink with me.

SOLYONY: Thrilled. (*They drink.*) I, Baron . . .

TUZENBACH: . . . yes?

SOLYONY: Have never nurtured the slightest complaint against you.

TUZENBACH: . . . no . . .

SOLYONY: But I possess . . . I possess . . .

TUZENBACH: . . . yes?

SOLYONY: . . . the *mien* . . . the *personality*, you see, of a *swashbuckler*.

TUZENBACH: . . . you do?

SOLYONY: . . . I am *impetuous* and *brash* . . . yes, I do . . . in my *manner*, in *demeanor* . . . I bear it in my face. Like *Lermontov*, whom, it is said, and I agree, I resemble, and who . . .

TUZENBACH: I'm resigning.

SOLYONY: You are?

TUZENBACH: I'm sending in my resignation. Today. Yes. I am. Five years I've been debating. And I've made up my mind, I am going to work. To *work*, you see . . .

SOLYONY (*declaiming*): "Be not embroiled in *Wrath*, Alekko, and Forswear thy dreams . . ."

(ANDREI *enters*.)

TUZENBACH: . . . I shall work.

SOLYONY: "For *Dreams* . . . for Dreams are but the . . ."

CHEBUTYKIN (*going into the parlor with* IRINA): You should have seen the meal they laid out. *Caucasian*. Absolutely Caucasian. Magnificent. Soup with *onions* . . . Cheremsha.

IRINA: . . . Cheremsha?

CHEBUTYKIN: A meat-and-potato stew . . .

SOLYONY: Burdock.

CHEBUTYKIN: Yes?

SOLYONY: A burdock stew.

CHEBUTYKIN: Yes?

SOLYONY: Burdock is not a meat. (*Pause*.) "*Burdock* . . ."

CHEBUTYKIN: Yes . . .

SOLYONY: Is a *plant*.

CHEBUTYKIN: *Burdock*.

SOLYONY: Yes. It's a plant, akin to the turnip.

CHEBUTYKIN: Yes. I know. *Cheremsha*, however.

SOLYONY: . . . yes?

CHEBUTYKIN: Is a lamb stew. (*Pause*.)

SOLYONY (*to himself*): Cheremsha is a lamb stew . . . (*To* CHEBUTYKIN:) But I am telling you that burdock . . .

CHEBUTYKIN: . . . yes . . . ?

SOLYONY: That *Cheremsha* is burdock.

CHEBUTYKIN: Yes, and I'm telling you that Cheremsha is lamb.

SOLYONY: And I'm telling *you* that Cheremsha is *burdock* and that burdock is a *plant*, and that Cheremsha is a plant, and it is burdock.

CHEBUTYKIN: And why should I, why should I dispute with *you*, who have never *been*, never *been* . . . have you ever been in the Caucasus . . . ?

SOLYONY: . . . I.

CHEBUTYKIN: Have you ever been in the Caucasus? You have never been in the Caucasus, and you have never *touched* Cheremsha.

SOLYONY: I've never *touched* it, as it is a turnip *stew,* a plant which I *detest,* the very *smell* of which . . .

ANDREI: Gentlemen . . .

SOLYONY: One moment . . . makes me nauseous, and I *ask* you, would I be *ignorant* of the *identity* of a substance which, the very *sight* of it, had the ability to cause me such distress?

CHEBUTYKIN: I . . .

SOLYONY: . . . seriously. I ask you.

ANDREI: Gentlemen.

SOLYONY: Your proposition's ludicrous upon the *face* of it.

NATALYA (*reentering*): . . . gentlemen . . . (*Exits.*)

SOLYONY: Respond to *that.*

ANDREI: Gentlemen. *Enough.* I beg you . . . *enough.*

TUZENBACH: When are the mummers coming?

IRINA: They promised by nine. Any time now.

TUZENBACH (*embraces* ANDREI *and sings and dances*): "Oh my bower, Oh my bower, Oh my bower new."

ANDREI (*singing and dancing*): "Bright paint and latticed maplewood."

CHEBUTYKIN: "Good strong and pleasant maplewood . . ."

TUZENBACH: Oh the *hell* with it. Let's just get drunk. Andriushka: let's drink *brüderschaft.* Let us drink to that. You and me. Andriushka. To Moscow. Yes. To the university!

SOLYONY: Which one?

TUZENBACH: What?

SOLYONY: Which one? (*Pause.*) Moscow has two universities. (*Pause.*)

ANDREI: Moscow has one university.

SOLYONY: And I'm telling you two.

ANDREI: Fine. Alright. Two, three, so much the better for Moscow.

SOLYONY: No. Two. Not three. Two. Being the number of universities in Moscow. The *old*, and the *new.* And if my words displease you, if they "irritate," you see, I needn't *stay*, I can *remove* myself. (*Exits.*)

TUZENBACH: Bravo. He outdoes his very self. Bravo, our own Solyony. Ladies and gentlemen, I'm sitting down to play.

MASHA: The baron's drunk . . .

TUZENBACH: I'm preparing to play . . .

MASHA: The baron's drunk, the baron's drunk, he's drunk.

(*Enter* NATALYA.)

NATALYA (*to* CHEBUTYKIN): Ivan Romanych . . . (*She says something to* CHEBUTYKIN, *then goes out quietly.*)

(CHEBUTYKIN *touches* TUZENBACH *on the shoulder, whispers something to him.*)

IRINA: What is it?

CHEBUTYKIN: Time to go. Take care.

IRINA: Ah. Yes. Oh. One moment . . . the mummers?

ANDREI: Oh. They've been canceled. (*Pause.*) Natalya, you see (*pause*) Natalya says Bobik is not well and, so, you see, *I* don't know . . . *I* don't care . . . it's all the same to me . . .

IRINA: . . . Bobik isn't well . . . ?

MASHA: Well, then the *hell* with it. We're kicked out, and we've *got* to *go.* Ain't that the thing of it? Companions . . . ? (*To* IRINA:) Saying that it's not our Bobik who is unwell, but someone else . . . isn't that so . . . ? (*Taps forehead.*) In this portion right here . . . the *shrew.*

(ANDREI *goes to his room through the door on the right.* CHEBUTYKIN *follows him. In the reception room people are saying goodbye.*)

FEDOTIK: What a pity. I was so counting on spending a lovely evening. (*Pause.*) But if the little thing is sick, of course. I'll bring something *by* for him tomorrow, a *"toy"* . . .

RODE: I *purposefully* took a long nap after dinner, as I'd intended to *dance* all night, it's nine *o'clock*, for the Lord's sake . . .

MASHA: . . . on the street. We'll hash it all out there.

(*Everyone exits.* CHEBUTYKIN *and* ANDREI *enter quietly.*)

CHEBUTYKIN: I had, had not *time* to marry. Life flashed by me like *lightning*. And . . . (*pause*) and I deeply loved your dear mother. Your mother, who, of course, *was* married . . . so . . .

ANDREI: Men shouldn't marry.

CHEBUTYKIN: No?

ANDREI: It's . . . (*Pause.*) It's boring.

CHEBUTYKIN: Is it?

ANDREI: Yes.

CHEBUTYKIN: Aha. (*Pause.*) The *other* hand . . .

ANDREI: Yes?

CHEBUTYKIN: Loneliness.

ANDREI: Mmm.

CHEBUTYKIN: Philosophize all you like. But *loneliness* . . . devastating. Do you see? Dear fellow. Yes. It is. Though, and in this, you're right; set one against the other, and what do you have?

ANDREI: Well.

CHEBUTYKIN: Yes.

ANDREI: Let's go now, shall we . . . ?

CHEBUTYKIN: All the time in the world.

ANDREI: Let's go now, though.

CHEBUTYKIN: Why?

ANDREI (*pause*): I don't want my wife to stop me going.

CHEBUTYKIN: Mmm.

ANDREI: No, no, no. I'm not going to play today. *No.* I'm not. I'm not *up* to it . . . that's *right*. (*Pause.*) Ivan Romanych.

CHEBUTYKIN: Yes.

ANDREI: What do I take for a shortness of breath?

CHEBUTYKIN: I don't *remember,* and I don't think that I ever knew.

ANDREI: Let's get out through the kitchen.

> (*They exit. A ring, another ring. Voices are heard offstage, laughter.*)

IRINA (*entering*): What's that, who's there . . . ?

ANFISA (*in a whisper*): The mummers.

IRINA: *Nanny.* Tell them there's no one home. Please ask them . . . (ANFISA *starts to exit*) . . . their pardon. (*Pause.*)

> (SOLYONY *enters.*)

SOLYONY: . . . why . . . why is . . . where is everyone . . . ?

IRINA: Gone home.

SOLYONY: Odd. (*Pause.*) Are you alone?

IRINA: Yes. (*Pause.*) Goodbye.

SOLYONY: You know, I believed I behaved, just now, without sufficient restraint. And that I acted tactlessly. But you can understand me. I feel that. You are so far above the average of . . . *intelligence*, of . . . you are *pure*. I think that you are *elevated*. You perceive the truth. And you, alone, can understand me. And my love. I *profoundly*, I *endlessly* . . . adore . . .

IRINA: Oh. Go away. (*Pause.*) Go away. *Goodbye.*

SOLYONY: . . . I cannot live without you. My angel. My *bliss*. My darling. You magnificent, you wonderful, such eyes, which no mortal . . .

IRINA: I said Stop It. (*Pause.*)

SOLYONY: I am speaking of my love for you. For the first time.

IRINA: . . . Vassily Vassilych . . .

SOLYONY: And, as I do, it is as if I am not on the earth. Or, I *am* on the earth, for, for the first time, and that, *previously* . . .

IRINA: VASSILY VASSILYCH . . . (*Pause.*)

SOLYONY: Yes. (*Pause.*) I see. One cannot make oneself dear to someone else by force. (*Pause.*) I see. (*Pause.*) Of course, yes. (*Pause.*) As long as there are no *rivals;* you see? For a *rival* is an obstacle which may be overcome. Eh? a *rival* . . . a rival may be *killed*, he may, my *God*, I love you. My *Bliss*, my . . .

(NATALYA *passes, with a candle. She looks behind one door and passes by the door, looking for her husband's room.*)

NATALYA: . . . weeellll, that's *Andrei*—let him read . . . Vassily Vassilych. I beg your pardon. Please excuse my undress. I didn't know you were still . . .

SOLYONY: . . . it's all one, believe me.

NATALYA: I . . .

SOLYONY: Goodbye . . . (*Exits.*)

NATALYA: You must be tired, my dear. Mmm? Ought to get you to bed earlier. Mmm . . .

IRINA: Is Bobik sleeping?

NATALYA: Asleep. Barely, but yes. Restlessly.

IRINA: Mmm.

NATALYA: I meant, by the way, dearest, I meant to bring it up to you, but you're *out*, or I've been *busy*, eh?

IRINA: Yes?

NATALYA: . . . but he's been *cold*, you see, in his room, Bobik . . . it seems to me. His *nursery* is always cold. It's damp, and your room would be so nice for a child. So warm, and would you do this and move into Olga's room for me . . . ? A little while. My dearest . . . ? (*Pause.*)

IRINA: What?

(*Sleighbells are heard approaching the house.*)

NATALYA: That you and Olga would move in together. In her room. A while. A little while. To give Bobik your room. For the warmth. My angel. I said to him today, "*Bobik:* You're *mine.* Mine. Mine. Mine." And he responded to me. With those eyes . . . ? You know? He looked at me. With those eyes of his. (*A ring.*) Well, mustn't that be *Olga*? Mmm. How late she is . . .

(*The maid goes up to* NATALYA, *whispers in her ear.*)

NATALYA: Protopopov . . . ? What a funny man! "*Protopopov*" has come. To ask me to go for a *troika* ride. Ha! How bizarre these men are. *Aren't* they . . . ? (*Pause.*) Aren't they . . . ? (*A ring.*) Someone's come. Yes. I suppose I *could* go riding—for a quarter hour. (*A ring.*) And that must be Olga.

(NATALYA *and the maid exit. Enter* KULYGIN, VERSHININ, *and* OLGA.)

KULYGIN: Well, *here's* one for you . . . said that they'd be having a soiree. What do you make of it . . . ?

VERSHININ: I left not half an hour ago, and the mummers were coming.

IRINA: Everyone's gone.

KULYGIN: Masha's gone, too? (*Pause.*) Where did she go? Protopopov's downstairs in a *troika*. (*Pause.*) Waiting for whom?

IRINA: Oh. Please. No questions. I'm so tired.

KULYGIN: Ah. You capricious girl.

OLGA: The meeting's just ended. I'm sick-tired. (*Pause.*) My head is splitting. The headmistress is ill. I'm doing *her* job . . . Andrei squandered two hundred fifty roubles at cards yesterday, the whole town's talking about it.

KULYGIN: . . . yes. I was tired by the meeting too.

VERSHININ: Well. The wife took a funny way to frighten me a bit. She's almost killed herself . . . (*Sighs.*) But it came 'round alright. So . . . well. (*Pause.*) And we're *resting* now . . . are we . . . ? No "soiree"? No. And, so, we're off, I suppose. Yes. Well, then, permit me to wish you the best. Fyodor Ilych . . . ? Will you come with me? We'll go somewhere. Eh? Can't go "home" mmm. No. Come with me.

KULYGIN: No.

VERSHININ: Please.

KULYGIN: I'm *exhausted*. No. I'm not coming. (*He gets up.*) Has my wife gone home?

IRINA: Must have.

KULYGIN (*kisses her hand*): Goodbye. Tomorrow, and the day after tomorrow. We can rest. Goodbye. I really need some tea. Thought we were going to spend the evening . . . (*Pause.*) Refreshments . . . oh well. *O fallacem hominum spem*. Which we find is the accusative case, exclamatory . . . (*Exits.*)

VERSHININ (*following*): I'll come too.

OLGA: Oh, *God*, my head. And Andrei has lost a fortune. And the whole *town's* gossiping about it. I have to lie down. Two days' rest. Tomorrow I'm free. And the day after tomorrow I'm free. Oh. My God. My head. Why do you do this to me . . . ? (*Exits.*)

IRINA: All gone.

NATALYA (*entering*): Just going out half an hour. Then I will be back. (*Exits.*)

IRINA (*pause*): Moscow. (*Pause.*) Oh, Lord. Could we go to Moscow . . .

Act III

Olga and Irina's room. To the left and right, screened off beds. It is past two o'clock in the morning. Outside, a fire alarm is being sounded. MASHA is lying on the couch in a black dress. Enter ANFISA and OLGA.

ANFISA: Well, now, they're under the stairs. "Have the Gracious Goodness to come up," I say. "Who *acts* like that . . . ?" And they say, "*Father.* Where *are* you . . . ? We don't know where he *is* . . ." God forbid. "He's *burned*" they say. "He's burned up!!!" How do they *think* these things? Out in the yard, we've got some there, too. *Also* uncovered. Undressed.

OLGA (*taking clothes out of the wardrobe*): Take . . . yes . . . take the little gray one. Take *this* one. Take the skirt, too, Nanny. Oh. My God. The whole of Kirsanovsky Lane's burnt down.

ANFISA: Lord.

OLGA: Burnt down to the ground. Take this one, too. The poor Vershinins. Nearly lost their house.

ANFISA: . . . God bless them . . .

OLGA: . . . and let them spend the night here.

ANFISA: Yes.

OLGA: Mustn't go home.

ANFISA: No.

OLGA: And poor Fedotik. Everything burnt. (*Pause.*) Quite lost.

ANFISA: Good if you called Ferapont.

OLGA: Mmm. Yes.

ANFISA: Or Oliushka, or I won't be able to carry it all.

OLGA (*sound of a ring*): Come in. Whoever is there . . .

(*Through the door the red glare of the fire is visible. The sound of a fire brigade passing is heard.*)

How horrible . . .

(*Enter* FERAPONT.)

Take this downstairs. The Kolotilin girls. They're standing under the stairs.

FERAPONT: Yes, miss.

OLGA: Give it to them.

FERAPONT: Yes, miss.

OLGA: Go.

FERAPONT: In the year twelve, Moscow was burnt too.

OLGA: . . . would . . . ?

FERAPONT: . . . was it *not*? Eh? And *weren't* the French surprised? We . . .

OLGA: Would you go, please?

FERAPONT: Yes, miss.

OLGA: Nanny.

ANFISA: Yes?

OLGA: Give it all away. We don't need any of it. Give it all away. Oh, Lord. I'm tired. I can hardly stand. Don't let the Vershinins go home. Put the girls in the parlor. Alexandr Ignatyevich can go down to the baron's room too. Or he can stay here. And the doctor is drunk, as it falls out, and must be alone . . . and Vershinin . . .

ANFISA: Yes . . . ?

OLGA: . . . his wife in the parlor too.

ANFISA: Oliushka, dear. (*Pause.*) Oliushka . . . (*Pause.*)

OLGA: Yes?

ANFISA: Oliushka.

OLGA: Yes.

ANFISA: Don't put me out.

OLGA: What?

ANFISA: Please don't put me out.

OLGA: What are you saying? No one's putting you out.

ANFISA: . . . my Golden Child, you know. I work and slave. I must grow weak, I'm "old," and everyone will say "Put her out. What good can she do?" But where would I go? Eighty-two years old, my next name day, and God willing that . . . "Go on, GO!" To an old woman . . . but, but . . .

OLGA: Nanny . . .

ANFISA: . . . where would I *go*?

OLGA: Nanny, dear, please. Please. You're tired. Rest. My good one. Shhhh. You're white as a . . . no one is putting you out.

(*Enter* NATALYA.)

NATALYA: Well. They're saying we should take up a subscription. For the victims. As we should. Right away. For the fire victims. Excellent idea. As the poor should be helped. It is the duty of the rich, and he who gives quickly gives twice. Bobik and Sofotchka are sleeping away. Just as if nothing had occurred. Aren't they . . . ? Oh. *Such* a lot of people in the house. Wherever one turns. And influenza in town and I'm terrified the children will get it.

OLGA (*looking out the window*): We can't see the fire from here. So peaceful.

NATALYA (*in front of a mirror*): Yes. I must look a fright. They say I've put on weight. Well. *That's* not true . . . No. Not a bit of it. And Masha sleeping. She's exhausted. *Isn't* she? . . . poor thing. (*To* ANFISA:) How *dare* you sit in my presence? How *dare* you??? Get up! Get out of here! Get UP!! (ANFISA *exits.*) HOW CAN YOU KEEP THAT HAG? I swear to the *Lord*, I don't understand you.

OLGA: . . . forgive me . . . what? (*Pause.*) What?

NATALYA: What *use* is she? Why is she *here*? She's . . . why is she here . . . ? She's a *peasant*, she shouldn't be in the house. She should be in the *country* somewhere. What are you "playing" at . . . ? A house must run on *order*. Like a *machine*. Do you understand? It cannot have a superfluous part. *You* understand me. Poor thing. Poor tired thing. Our headmistress is tired. Yessss. When my Sofotchka grows up and goes to the academy, then I must live in fear of you. *Won't* I . . . ?

OLGA: I won't be the headmistress.

NATALYA: Yes. You will. Olyetchka. It's been decided.

OLGA: It's beyond me.

NATALYA: What?

OLGA: I shall decline.

NATALYA: Why?

OLGA: I can't. It's beyond my strength. (*Pause.*) You were so rude to Nanny just now . . . I . . . forgive me . . . I'm . . . I don't have the *strength* . . . to *endure* . . . it all went dark. For one moment.

NATALYA: Oh, God. Olga. Forgive me. I'm sorry.

OLGA: . . . it . . .

NATALYA: . . . so sorry I've *upset* you . . .

OLGA: We, if you would understand me, we were brought up strangely. It's true, but I cannot bear, bear to see such treatment. I can't *bear* it. Do you hear me? It makes me *heartsick* . . .

NATALYA: I'm sorry, I . . .

OLGA: . . . the slightest rudeness. A harsh word, a thoughtless word . . .

NATALYA: I often say what's uncalled for. It's true.

OLGA: . . . it so *disturbs* me . . .

NATALYA: But you must agree, my dear, she really should live in the country.

OLGA: She's been with us thirty years.

NATALYA: But she cannot *work* anymore. I don't . . . I, I don't understand it. Either I don't understand or you don't wish me to. She cannot *work* anymore. She just sleeps or sits.

OLGA: Let her sit, then.

NATALYA: What do you mean?

OLGA: Let her sit.

NATALYA: But she's a *servant.* (*Pause.*) I don't *understand* you, Olga. I don't *understand* you. I have a maid. I have a *nanny* . . . I have a wet nurse . . . why in the world would we need this old *woman* . . . ? *Why.* What *for?*

(*Sound of an alarm offstage.*)

OLGA: I've aged ten years tonight.

NATALYA: *Olga.* (*Pause.*) It's essential for us to come to an understanding. You're at the academy all day. While I am at the house. (*Pause.*) You have your *teaching.* I have my *domestic* duties. If I say something touching the help . . . (*Pause.*) If I say something treating of the *help* . . . then I know what I'm speaking of. Do you understand me? And I want her gone. I want her to be out of here. By tomorrow night. *OUT* of here. I'm here all day, and I say so. That *hag.* She's a *thief* . . . she's . . . I know what she is. You don't. YOU AREN'T HERE. And I won't have you, I will not *stand* for this behavior on your part. Do you . . . (*Pause.*) You know . . . really . . . I think if you don't move downstairs we are likely always to be quarreling. Don't you think? It's not right.

(*Enter* KULYGIN.)

KULYGIN: Where's Masha? It's time to go home. The fire's dying down. They say. (*Stretches.*) Only one block lost. What a wind, though. We thought the whole town would go. Oh, Lord, I'm tired. Olyetchka, my dear, you know, often I've thought, if it wasn't Masha, I'd have married *you* . . . you are so good . . . (*Pause.*) I'm tired to my bones. (*He listens.*)

OLGA: What?

KULYGIN: Seems that our doctor's on a, somewhat of a *bender*. And it seems he's coming here . . . yes? Hear it? *Oh* yes. Alright. (*Pause.*) Don't give me away. (*He starts to hide himself in the wardrobe. To himself:*) Our *doctor* . . .

OLGA: Two years he hasn't been drinking.

KULYGIN: Mmm . . .

OLGA: . . . all of a sudden now . . .

   (CHEBUTYKIN *enters, goes to the washstand, and starts washing his hands.*)

CHEBUTYKIN: The devil, the devil, the devil "take" them. Take the *lot* of them. What do they think I am. "A doctor." What am I supposed to do? Well. He's supposed to *recognize* and *treat* and *cure* all sorts of . . . what? *Disease* and *maladies.* While I know absolutely nothing. I remember nothing, if I learnt it, and I *know* nothing.

   (OLGA *and* NATALYA *exit.*)

Last Wednesday. The woman in Zasp. The doctor treated her. She died. It was my fault. Twenty-five *years* ago . . . Yes. Yes. *Then.* But now? I am nothing. What am I?

Nothing. No profession. And no arms. No legs. Nothing. Not a man. Not a man. But not to *exist* . . . Dear Lord, forgive me and the people at the club. Talking of *Shakespeare, Werther* . . . talking of them . . . talking to me of them. *I* haven't read them. And yet I'm nodding at them. I'm nodding at them. Why? WHY IN THE WORLD AM I PRETENDING? *WHY?* That woman? I *butchered* her. I killed her. *All* of it. How can one sort it out? How? When one is *puking* at the *sordidness* of this life. This loathsome *self*, leading a life . . . and so I started drinking . . .

(IRINA, VERSHININ, *and* TUZENBACH *enter.* TUZENBACH *is wearing civilian clothes, very new.*)

IRINA: We can sit here. No one will come in here.

VERSHININ: The soldiers saved the town.

IRINA: Yes.

VERSHININ: Weren't for the soldiers, the town would have burnt. Good. Good men. Lovely men.

KULYGIN: Ladies and gentlemen. What is the hour?

TUZENBACH: Going on four.

KULYGIN: Mmm.

TUZENBACH: Getting light soon.

IRINA: Everyone's in the reception room. Nobody's going home. And your Solyony's in there too. Doctor. You ought to be in bed.

CHEBUTYKIN: Quite right, miss. (*Pause.*) Quite right.

IRINA: . . . yes.

CHEBUTYKIN: *Thank* you, miss.

KULYGIN: Got swackered. Yes. You did. Ivan Romanych. *Good* boy. Good for you. That's my lad! *Vino veritas*, as the Old Folks explained it.

TUZENBACH: Everyone's asking me to engineer a benefit for the fire victims.

IRINA: How would we?

TUZENBACH: No—no, it could be done. If we wanted to do it.

IRINA: We . . .

TUZENBACH: Maria Sergeyevna plays the piano. She plays superbly.

KULYGIN: Superbly.

IRINA: . . . she . . .

KULYGIN: . . . like twenty angels.

IRINA: She hasn't touched the piano in years.

TUZENBACH: . . . no, I.

IRINA: For years.

TUZENBACH: No, I . . . I . . . this is not a musical town. It is not a town "schooled in music," but I give you my word that *she*, you see, plays magnificently. She does.

IRINA: Maria Sergeyevna.

TUZENBACH: Almost on a professional level.

KULYGIN: I love her, Baron. I love her. Masha. She is so.

TUZENBACH: . . . what must that be? To be so *gifted*. To play so . . . "well." And know that no one can appreciate it. What must that be like?

KULYGIN: Yes. She plays well. But.

TUZENBACH: . . . she does.

KULYGIN: . . . would it be proper? For her to take part? In a concert?

TUZENBACH (*pause*): Why not?

KULYGIN: Well, what do I know. Perhaps it would be fine. Perhaps. I don't know anything. You see. What do I know? But our headmaster . . . a fine man, an intelligent man . . . he has such "views." Do you understand me? And, it is not "his business," of course, but perhaps I could refer it to him . . .

(CHEBUTYKIN *picks up and examines a peculiar clock.*)

VERSHININ: I got all filthy at the fire. I look like something. What do I look like? Nothing on earth. I heard yesterday. There is talk that they may transfer the brigade. Yes. To *Poland*, perhaps, or China.

TUZENBACH: Yes. I heard that too.

VERSHININ: Mmm.

TUZENBACH: *That* would empty the town . . .

IRINA: . . . and we would be going away too . . .

(CHEBUTYKIN *drops the clock.*)

CHEBUTYKIN: Smashed to flinders. (*Pause.*)

KULYGIN: Zero for conduct, Ivan Romanych.

IRINA: That was Mama's clock.

CHEBUTYKIN: Perhaps. Perhaps that was Mama's clock. And perhaps it was hers and perhaps it appears that I broke it. Perhaps it *seems* that I did. And perhaps we do not exist—to think these things. And if we did not think them, do *they* exist? Do they? And is it not true that no one knows *anything*, finally? Is that not the case? (*By the door.*) What are you looking at? Natalya's in there flirting with Protopopov. *You* don't see it. You're in *here.* She's in *there.* That's the nature of phenomena. She's in there. Flirting with Protopopov. Would you find it diverting to accept this little *plum* . . . ?

VERSHININ: Thank you. (*Laughs.*) How *odd* this all is, finally.

CHEBUTYKIN: Mmm.

VERSHININ: I ran home. When the fire broke out. I raced home. As I got there, I saw the house was safe. But my girls, my little girls—they were out on the threshold. Dressed in their thin underclothes. Their mother wasn't there. Everywhere people running. Horses, dogs running . . . I saw on their faces such terror. Such terror. It broke my heart. My *God*, the things those little girls will have to face in the course of their lives. (*Pause.*) What they will have to live through. And I came here. (*Pause.*) And here is their mother. (*Alarm.*) My little girls. Were stranded at the threshold.

(MASHA *enters, sits.*)

And the street was red with fire. And there was. That terrible noise. And I thought: long ago . . . long ago . . . that *something like this* has occurred. (*Pause.*) There was a raid. An enemy . . . "invaded" . . . they looted. And killed and plundered. (*Pause.*) In a savage time. And I thought: in essence, what difference is there? Between that time and this? Between that and this. (*Pause.*) Between what *was* and *is* . . . ? And then more time will pass. Two, and three hundred years. Will have passed. And *our* life. Our . . . "shouting" . . . will be looked back on with the same . . . "incredulity" as that which *we* have. Looking at the past. How odd it seems. How *awkward*. How strange. (*Pause.*) Yes. Forgive me. It seems that I'm "going on again." I am philosophizing. (*Pause.*) Listen to me. It seems . . . what if . . . as if everyone in the town were sleeping. Can you feel that? As if that were so? As if only we three in the town were awake. Truly awake. But. In each generation. As time passed. More would come. Gradually. Constantly. Until the *people*, you see, gradually, would come 'round to think your way. Until this state of "wakefulness," over the years, until it came to be, you see . . . the "norm." Until that norm *itself* was surpassed. In "time" . . . do you see . . . ? In "time" . . . and people. Who were born. Looked back . . . they looked back . . . (*Pause.*) Ha. (*Pause.*) *Lord*, I want to live . . . I'm in a mood, I know it . . . I would like to live to see it . . . *HA*. But I want to live . . . (*Sings.*) "All ages are in thrall to love. The very spheres Adore her."

(MASHA *sings along with him a bit. Enter* FEDOTIK, *who sings along and dances.*)

FEDOTIK: "Burnt *Out*, Burnt *Down*, burnt out all *Around* . . ." (*Pause.*) Quite completely burnt.

IRINA: Why are you singing about it?

FEDOTIK: . . . quite completely burnt. All gone. Guitar's gone. All of the photographs burnt. All of my letters. I wanted to give you one of my notebooks. (*Sighs*.) They're all burnt too.

(*Enter* SOLYONY.)

IRINA: No. No, please. Vassily Vassilych, *please*. Not now.

SOLYONY: I . . .

IRINA: You . . . you can't come in.

SOLYONY: . . . I can't come in . . .

IRINA: No.

SOLYONY: The baron can. The baron can come in, but I can't . . . ?

VERSHININ: Well, I have to go in any case. How are they doing with the fire?

SOLYONY: It's subsiding.

VERSHININ: . . . Mmm.

SOLYONY: They say. No. I'm sorry. I find it *odd*. How is it that the *baron* comes in, and I can't?

VERSHININ (*singing*): ta tum ta tum ta tum ta tum . . . the very Spheres.

(MASHA *sings along with him*.)

VERSHININ (*to* SOLYONY): We'll go in to the foyer.

SOLYONY: Well. Fine. If that's the answer. "Yes. It all could be a bit more clear. But that would irk the Geese, I fear . . ."

(*He makes clucking noises at* TUZENBACH. *Exits with* VERSHININ *and* FEDOTIK.)

IRINA: Solyony has smoked up the room. The baron's asleep. Baron! . . . the baron's asleep.

TUZENBACH: . . . waking. Oh, God I'm tired. (*Pause.*) The brickyard. You see, that's a day's work. I'm not joking with you. And I don't say it in jest. I *will* be working. In the brickyard, soon. I've already been speaking to a man. (*To* IRINA:) You are so pale. Do you know? You enchant me. *So* beautiful. Your pale complexion lightens the dark air. How sad you are. I see it in your face. Yes. You are sad. My darling. You are discontented. Discontented with life. Live with me. Come with me, *work* with me. Live with me . . .

MASHA: Nikolai Lvovich.

TUZENBACH: Yes.

MASHA: Get out of here.

TUZENBACH (*laughs*): *There* you are.

MASHA: Yes.

TUZENBACH: Alright. Oh, Lord. Alright. I'm going. Goodbye, I look at you now, and the *past* comes back to me. I see you *long* ago. Long ago on your *birthday.* So long ago. Bright. Young. You spoke of the "joys of Labor." Yes, you did. And how *right* life seemed to me then. How *right* it seemed. That Happy Life. You're crying. Off you go. Go to bed, now. It's morning. It's almost light. The new day is coming. Oh. If I could give my life to you . . . (*Pause.*) I *give* it! Yes!

MASHA: Nikolai Lvovich.

TUZENBACH: Yes?

MASHA: That's enough.

TUZENBACH: Yes?

MASHA: Yes. Go away.

TUZENBACH: I'm going. (*Exits.*)

MASHA: Fyodor?

KULYGIN: Mmm.

MASHA: Are you sleeping?

KULYGIN: Eh?

MASHA: Go home. You ought to go home.

KULYGIN: My dear, sweet Masha. Dear girl . . .

IRINA: She's exhausted.

KULYGIN: . . . mmm?

IRINA: *Fedya* . . .

KULYGIN: Yes.

IRINA: Go and let her rest.

KULYGIN: Yes. In a moment. *My. Good. Wife.* My only one. My nice "wife." I love you, my . . .

MASHA: *Amo. Amas. Amat. Amamus, amatis, amant.*

KULYGIN: Isn't it. You amaze me. Seven years of marriage and it seems to me that we met *yesterday. Yesterday,* eh? Seven years. And what a woman. What am I? *Content.* Yes. That is the world which we're speaking of. A man who is content. Who . . .

MASHA: And I'm sick. I'm sick. I'm tired. A woman who is both, and are you listening. *Tired* and *sick.* And what else? What else has been done? To *plague* me, and to occupy my *thoughts* . . . with *worry.* All day. Every day, a nail in my shoe: he's mortgaged the house, Andrei. Our Andriushka. Has mortgaged our *house.* The house where the *four* of us live. He mortgaged it. His wife's taken the money . . . FROM OUR HOUSE—which belongs, not to him alone, but to the *four* of us; and she's taken the money. How . . . how can an honest man . . .

KULYGIN: Shhhh, Masha . . .

MASHA: *What?*

KULYGIN: . . . why . . .

MASHA: Why *what?*

KULYGIN: He's in *debt*. Andriushka's in *debt*. He owes . . .

MASHA: He's in "debt" is he . . .?

KULYGIN: What do you need it for?

MASHA: What do I need it for? *What?*

KULYGIN: The money.

MASHA: It's *mine*. (*Pause.*) It's mine.

KULYGIN: Are we poor? Eh? I work. I teach. I give *lessons*. We have a good life. An honest life. Your needs . . .

MASHA: I wasn't speaking of our needs.

KULYGIN: What are you speaking of?

MASHA: I'm speaking of injustice. (*Pause.*) Go, Fyodor. Go.

KULYGIN (*kisses her*): You're tired.

MASHA: I told you that.

KULYGIN: You rest. Rest a half hour or so. I'll wait for you. I'll sit out there. You rest. Sleep. I am content. I'll wait for you. (*Exiting.*) Oh, yes . . .

IRINA: How petty Andrei has become. How small. He is

wrung out by that woman. He was going to be a *professor.* Now he's boasting that he's been accepted as a member of the District Board. A member of the Wondrous Board. Of which board Protopopov is the chairman. And our Andrei's all elated he's a member of the ranks. The whole town's laughing at him. He sees nothing. And *here:* everyone is running to the fire. Where is our Andrei . . . ? In his room. Tuning his fiddle. Oh. Oh. I can't bear it any more. No. Please. I can't.

(OLGA *enters.*)

Put me out. Put me out. Put me out of here. I can't *bear* it.

OLGA: What *is* it? *Darling.* What *is* it . . . ?

IRINA: Where has it all gone? My *God*, where has it gone? I've lost *everything*. Where has it gone? It's lost in my head. I . . . I keep forgetting . . . I . . . the Italian for "window," for "ceiling" . . . HOW CAN I HAVE LOST IT? And life is passing. Every day. And *everything* we have is going by. And we will never go to Moscow. I see we won't go.

OLGA: . . . my dear . . .

IRINA: Oh! My unhappy life. I can't work anymore. I can't work anymore. I worked at the telegraph. And now I'm in an office. For the town. I hate my useless work. I hate it. I hate it. I'm almost twenty-four. I've been working so long. I've grown old working. I'm so tired. My brain is tired. My memory. I've become thin. And ugly. My mind has grown old. And nothing pleases me. Time passes. I feel myself . . . moving "off" from it. Farther and farther. From a beautiful life. Into some . . . (*Pause.*)

Why am I still alive? Why haven't I ended it? I don't understand, I . . .

OLGA: Shhhh. Darling. Don't cry. Shhhh. You're killing me.

IRINA: I'm not crying. I'm not. Now . . . now . . . No. I'm not crying anymore. I'm done.

OLGA: . . . my darling.

IRINA: . . . I . . .

OLGA: My darling. I tell you. I'm telling you. As a sister— I'm telling you. As your best friend: (*pause*) marry the baron. (*Pause.*) You respect him. You do. You "value" him. And it is *true:* he isn't handsome. But he's good. He's decent. And he's pure . . . as you know. Shhhh. Why . . . yes . . . why do we marry? For "love"? I think not. Finally, no. For *duty.* Yes. I think, in any case, that *I* would. Without love . . . ? Yes. *Whomever.* If he was decent. If he was *pure* . . . an *old* man, even. Yes. For the *important* thing . . .

IRINA: You know . . . I just keep waiting. I just kept on. Waiting for our move. "In *Moscow,*" I thought. "I'd meet my *real* man." My "destined" man. I dreamed of him. I loved him. I waited for him . . . what stupid folly.

OLGA (*embraces her*): I know. I know. I know. My darling. My *dear.* I know. (*Pause.*) I know. When the baron resigned and came to us without his uniform . . .

IRINA: . . . yes.

OLGA: I know . . . he looked so *dowdy* . . .

IRINA: . . . yes.

OLGA: . . . so dowdy. I started crying. What could I say to

him? "Why are you crying?" he said. But, but . . . wait a
moment. Darling . . . *"But."* If this good man, if this
"decent" man should want to *marry* you, I would be
happy. I would be so happy. Because, you see, this is
different . . . you see . . . because . . .

(NATALYA, *carrying a candle, enters and walks across
the stage.*)

MASHA: I think she set the fire.

OLGA: Oh *Masha* . . .

MASHA: . . . Mmm.

OLGA: You're the family clown.

MASHA: Mmm. My sisters? My Clown Soul. My Jolly Soul
is heavy, do you want to know? It is. Hear my confes-
sion. For I am in torment and my Guilty Knowledge
sears my Heart. My sinful Mystery. My secret which
screams to be told. I am in love and I love someone. I
love a man. You have just seen him. The man that I love.
Vershinin.

OLGA: Stop it.

MASHA: I . . .

OLGA: Stop it. I don't want to hear it.

MASHA: What am I to do? You tell me. He was *strange* to
me. At first. I *thought* about him. Often. I felt sorry for
him. I . . . I "grew to love him." I did. I grew to love him.
His *voice* . . . his *ways* . . . his *misfortunes* . . . his two
little *girls* . . .

OLGA: No no *no!* I can't hear. I Cannot Hear What You Are
Saying. *NO*. It's *shameful*. It's *foolishness*. I won't hear it.

MASHA: You won't hear it? Olga? You won't hear it? Why? I love him. He loves me. It's my Fate, do you see? This love. It's as simple as that. Yes. Yes, it's frightening. Yes. But it's *mine*. It's what I *am*. Yes. My darling. Yes. It's *life* s'what it is. We *live* it, and look what it does to us. We read a novel, and it's clear. It's so *spelled out*. This *isn't* clear. *Nothing* is clear. And *no* one has a final *true* idea of anything. It's "life." We have to *decide*. Each of us. We. Have. To *DECIDE*: what *is*, what it *means*, what we *want*. My darling sisters. (*Pause*.) That's what the thing is. And now I've confessed. And I'll be silent. (*Pause*.) As the grave. (*Pause*.) Silence.

(*Enter* ANDREI, *followed by* FERAPONT.)

ANDREI: *What?* I don't understand you.

FERAPONT: Andrei Sergeyevich. I have explained it to you. Ten times. I . . .

ANDREI: One moment. *Firstly:* you may call me "Your Honor."

FERAPONT: Andrei Ser . . .

ANDREI: *Not* Andrei Sergeyevich . . .

FERAPONT: . . . I . . .

ANDREI: "Your *Honor*."

FERAPONT: I . . .

ANDREI: "Your *Honor*." (*Pause*.)

FERAPONT: Your Honor . . . Your Honor. The firemen. Asking permission to get down to the river through the garden. (*Pause*.) They want to cut across the garden, else they'll have to go around—the . . . uh . . . "long way."

ANDREI: Alright. Tell them yes. (*Pause.* FERAPONT *does not leave.*) Al*right!* (FERAPONT *exits.*) *God,* am I sick of the . . . Where's Olga? (OLGA *comes out from behind a screen.*) I need you. Where is your key to the cupboard? That little key . . . ? (*She hands him the key.* IRINA *goes behind the screen.*) *Vast.* Vast fire. Overwhelming. Burning down now. Burning itself out. (*Pause.*) Ferapont. Fine, now I've gotten myself, made a fool of myself, n'front of him. "Your Honor." What is it? Olga? What is it? Let's have it out. It's enough, now. All of this, all of this "sulking," any moment . . . What is it? What have I done to you?

VERSHININ (*offstage, singing*): Tra traaa tra traaa . . .

MASHA (*getting up*): Tra traaa tra traaa. Olga: good*bye.* And God be with you. (*Kisses* IRINA, *goes behind the screen.*) All Restful Slumbers. Andrei: Goodbye. Goodbye. Leave us now. Everyone's so tired. You, you "have it out" tomorrow. (*Exits.*)

OLGA: Andriushka. Yes. Leave it til tomorrow. (*Goes behind the screen.*) Sleep now. Time to sleep.

ANDREI: No. I'll go. But I'm going to say it first. One moment. Please. Please. Firstly: my wife. You . . . please . . . there's something which you bear against her. Natalya. *I've* seen it. Since our wedding. Now: now: now: my wife, Natalya is, in my opinion, a fine human being. Can I say that plainer? A fine, honest, and straightforward, noble Human Being. I *respect* her, I respect those things in her, and I demand, I *demand* that others do the same. Do you see? She, my wife, is a "good woman," and all of your, your, your "grievances" against her, are, what can I call them? "whims." Now: suddenly, what? You seem to be "hurt." You're "grieved" at *my* life. That I have not, that I am not a "*professor*," that I do not occupy my life among the "sciences" . . . this angers you. My choices. My . . . as you perceive it, "*degradation*" in my choice of work. And this *reflects* upon you. Is that it? That . . . yes. Well, I've *said* it. But I *do* work. I *do* work. Don't I? I work on the District Council. As a member of the Board. And I am proud of that work, if you want to know. And don't *require* your . . . "endorsement" of that work to be proud of it. And, as it seems, you must *withhold* that, be it so. *Thirdly*, I have mortgaged the house. And I have done so, yes, without resort to your opinion. In this I am at fault, and I ask your pardon. (*Pause.*) I was compelled to it. By debt. (*Pause.*) I . . . uh . . . I . . . a debt, a debt of thirty-five thousand roubles. (*Pause.*) I no longer play at cards—you may have remarked. That I quit that some time since. (*Pause.*) If I, and if I may suggest something. To justify myself. Perhaps. That it was in my thoughts, as it *is*, that you girls, you are the guaranteed recipients of *income*, in the form of your *annuity*. While I, as you know, as you know, have nothing. *No* . . . "income" . . . no . . .

KULYGIN (*entering*): Is *Masha* here? No . . . ? Where is *Masha* . . . ? (*Exits.*)

ANDREI: . . . and Natalya, as I have said, is an *excellent* human being. She has a good soul. She . . . (*Pause.*) She . . . (*Pause.*) My darlings. (*Pause.*) My darling sisters. I thought that we'd be happy. (*Pause.*) I didn't marry her to be unhappy. I swear to you . . . I thought . . . my darlings . . . I . . . (*He weeps. Exits.*)

KULYGIN (*reentering*): No? She's not here? Where *is* she . . . ? Where the devil . . . ? (*Exits.*)

(*The stage is empty. Sound of an alarm. Sound of knocking.*)

IRINA (*behind the screen*): Olga . . . What is that?

OLGA: It's Doctor Ivan Romanych.

IRINA: *What?*

OLGA: It's Doctor Ivan Romanych. Knocking on the floor.

IRINA: Why is he doing that?

OLGA: He's drunk.

IRINA: . . . what a night. (*Pause.*)

OLGA: *What?*

IRINA (*looks out from behind the screen*): Olga . . .

OLGA: What?

IRINA: Did you hear?

OLGA: . . . did I . . . ?

IRINA: . . . that the brigade is being transferred.

OLGA: I heard it. Yes. It's only gossip.

IRINA: . . . because we'd be all alone. (*Pause.*) Olga.

OLGA: Yes.

IRINA: We'd be all alone. (*Pause.*) Olga.

OLGA: Yes.

IRINA: Olga . . . (*Pause.*) The *baron* . . .

OLGA: Yes. The baron?

IRINA: He is a good man?

OLGA: Yes.

IRINA: He's a good man. (*Pause.*) I can marry him.

OLGA: Yes?

IRINA: I'll marry him.

OLGA: You will.

IRINA: I'll agree to marry him. Only. Can we go to Moscow? Can we leave here? Olga? Please (*Pause.*) Olga . . .

Act IV

The old garden of the Prozoroff house. A long avenue of firs, at the end of which a river is visible. On the other side of the river, a forest. On the right, the terrace of the house; here, bottles and glasses on the table—it is evident that champagne has just been drunk. It is twelve o'clock noon. From the street, passersby walk through the garden to the river occasionally; five or so soldiers walk through rapidly.

CHEBUTYKIN, *in a benign mood which does not leave him throughout the entire act, is sitting in an armchair in the garden waiting to be called; he is in a military cap and has a stick.* IRINA, KULYGIN, *with a decoration around his neck and no moustache, and* TUZENBACH, *standing on the terrace, are seeing off* FEDOTIK *and* RODE, *who are walking down the steps; both officers are in field dress.*

TUZENBACH (*exchanges kisses with* FEDOTIK): You are a good man. You are a good man. *Such* a pleasure. Knowing you. (*Goes to* RODE. *Exchanges kisses.*) One more time. My dear. Farewell.

87

IRINA: Goodbye.

FEDOTIK: Yes. Farewell. Not goodbye, but farewell. For we will not meet again.

KULYGIN: Who can say? Who can say . . . Oh, Lord . . . I've started crying too.

IRINA: . . . *someday* . . .

FEDOTIK: Ten years? Fifteen years from now? Who will we be then? Wait . . . wait . . . wait . . . (*Takes a snapshot.*) Just once more . . .

RODE (*embraces* TUZENBACH): No. We shall not meet again. (*Kisses Irina's hand.*) Thank you. For everything.

FEDOTIK: Please. Just a moment. Will you . . . ?

TUZENBACH: No. We'll meet again. God willing . . . *write* us . . .

RODE: . . . yes.

TUZENBACH: No. Truly. *Write* to us.

RODE: Farewell. *Trees,* farewell. *Air,* farewell, *Echo* . . . echo . . . farewell . . .

KULYGIN: And who's to say? You may get *married* there . . .

RODE: . . . in Poland . . . ?

KULYGIN: Yes. Why not? A Polish wife. To embrace you, to call you *Kokhaneh* . . .

FEDOTIK (*glances at his watch*): Hour left. One. Hour. Left. Less. Out of our battery, only Solyony's trav'ling on the barge. And we are going with the combat unit. Hmm. Three of the companies are off today. And tomorrow the remaining three. And then the town will be at peace. Will be Left at Peace.

TUZENBACH: And unrelieved boredom.

RODE: Where is Maria Sergeyevna?

KULYGIN: In the garden.

FEDOTIK: We should tell her we're off.

RODE: . . . farewell.

FEDOTIK: Tell her we said goodbye.

RODE: I'm off, or else I'm going, to, I'm going to break down weeping. I am. (*Embraces* TUZENBACH *and* KULYGIN. *Kisses Irina's hand.*) Our life here has been so . . .

FEDOTIK (*to* KULYGIN): This is for you . . . (*Hands him several items.*)

RODE: . . . it has been *splendid*.

FEDOTIK (*to* KULYGIN): A souvenir.

RODE (*to himself*): . . . splendid.

FEDOTIK: . . . little *notebook,* and a *pencil* . . . well. Let's get down to the barge. (*They exit.*)

RODE (*shouting*): Yo!

KULYGIN (*pause, shouts*): Farewell.

(*At the rear of the stage,* FEDOTIK *and* RODE *meet* MASHA *and go out with her.*)

IRINA: . . . and gone.

CHEBUTYKIN: Gone. And who said goodbye to me?

IRINA: And what did you say to *them* . . . ?

CHEBUTYKIN: I forgot.

IRINA: Mmm.

CHEBUTYKIN: Well. I did. (*Shrugs.*) I'll see them soon. (*Pause.*) I'm off tomorrow too. One little day. One more day. One more year til my retirement. And then I'll return. And live out my life here. Near you. One more year til my pension. And an *involutional* change in my life. Into a life so . . . *quiet.* So "retired." Obliging, *genteel.*

IRINA: Yes. You change your life here. (*Pause.*) Yes. You should do that.

CHEBUTYKIN: Yes. One feels one should . . .

IRINA: . . . my dear.

CHEBUTYKIN (*sings*): Tra traaa . . . tra traaa . . . "Upon this Rock you Find me . . ."

KULYGIN: Ivan Romanych . . . ?

CHEBUTYKIN: *Oh* yes . . . ?

KULYGIN: What can one do with you?

CHEBUTYKIN: Nothing. (*Pause.*) And very little of *that.*

IRINA: Fyodor's shaved his moustache. I can't bear to look at him.

KULYGIN: Why?

CHEBUTYKIN: Well. We see what your *face* looks like.

KULYGIN: Mmm.

CHEBUTYKIN: Why'd'ja do it?

KULYGIN: It's the "thing," I believe.

CHEBUTYKIN: Mmm . . . ?

KULYGIN: Headmaster's shaved his moustache. Made me an under head, and mine went too. Nobody likes it.

CHEBUTYKIN: Doesn't suit you.

KULYGIN: No. But it is "the done thing." And, so, there you are.

(*At the rear of the stage,* ANDREI *is wheeling a baby carriage.*)

IRINA: Ivan *Romanych* . . .

CHEBUTYKIN: Your servant.

IRINA: I'm concerned.

CHEBUTYKIN: For what?

IRINA: I'm worried.

CHEBUTYKIN: Of what?

IRINA: Yesterday . . .

CHEBUTYKIN: . . . yes . . . ?

IRINA: When you were *walking*. What transpired.

CHEBUTYKIN: "Transpired."

IRINA: Yes.

CHEBUTYKIN: Nothing.

IRINA: Nothing?

CHEBUTYKIN: No.

IRINA: No? On the boulevard . . . ?

CHEBUTYKIN: The boulevard?

IRINA: Yes.

CHEBUTYKIN: Nothing. (*Reads the paper.*) No—nothing, all the same . . .

KULYGIN: They're saying that Solyony and the baron.

CHEBUTYKIN (*reading*): Mmm hmm . . .

KULYGIN: "Met" yesterday . . .

CHEBUTYKIN: . . . Mmm . . .

KULYGIN: On the boulevard.

CHEBUTYKIN: Yes . . .

KULYGIN: Near the theatre. And apparently.

TUZENBACH: Oh, please. *Enough* of that now. (*Goes into the house.*)

KULYGIN: Apparently . . . apparently Solyony took it on himself to *taunt* the baron . . . to . . . "taunt" him. And he, the baron, took "offense." And "said" something, which Solyony . . .

CHEBUTYKIN: . . . what stupid gossip.

KULYGIN: D'you know that that derives from "God's Sibs," which is to say "siblings," which is the name given to the midwives of the seventeenth century. In England. *Of* which profession the brother of a quite good friend of mine wrote a doctoral dissertation while we were at university, which paper I was privileged to read and find quite the most boring compendium it has ever fallen to my lot to see. They say Solyony is in love with Irina, and he has, understandably, then, come to loathe the baron. A fine girl. Irina. Not unlike my Masha. No. Giv'n to *reflection*, you are, with, though, as we know, a gentler disposition . . . well, no, though, then, again, then, Masha, to be just, her disposition can be quite, I, I adore her, Masha.

(*At the rear of the garden, offstage,* Coo-eeeee, Coo-
eeeee!)

IRINA (*shudders*): Huh. It all frightens me today. (*Sighs.*)
I'm packed. And they're coming. After dinner. To pick
up my things. And tomorrow, too. I shall be Married.
And the baron and I will be off. And the day after I will
be already "installed" at the school, and won't that be
the start of a New Life. With God's help. I sat for the
teacher's examination and I cried at the awesome "com-
pletion" of it all. (*Pause.*) They'll be coming here for the
things soon.

KULYGIN: Hmm. (*Pause.*) *However* it may be, for, finally,
what is "philosophy," and what is "talk"? However:
from the bottom of My Heart, I wish it to you.

CHEBUTYKIN: Quite moving. My good Golden Girl. All of
you. Come so far. Grown so. Who can keep pace with
you? Not one who has been left behind. No. Like the
old bird when the young birds fly. Well, fly, then, my
dear darlings. What else is it all for? Fyodor Ilych—you
were a fool to shave your moustache.

KULYGIN: Thank you. (*Sighs.*) The military, today, will
have mustered and decamped. And everything will go
on. As it did before they came. And Masha is a *fine*
woman. A *good* woman. *Whatever* they may say; and
who is there that has not had everything said about
them, in the course of a full life? I love her. And I thank
the fate which bore me to her. *People* . . . (*pause*) have
different destinies. Within the *excise* office, we discover
a certain *Kozyrioff*. He was at school with me. He was
"sent down." As he could never come to terms with
certain peculiarities of the Latin tongue. He is now
fallen on Hard Times. I, when I see him, have been

known to greet him thus: "Hail, *ut consecutivum!*" To which, when done, he replies: "Yes. *Ut consecutivum* precisely." He adds his thanks. He coughs a bit. A fellow in a bad way, no mistake about it. While I, on the other hand, may stand as an example to the contrary, and the reasons being what they may, of a man who all his life has enjoyed quite a good degree of Luck. And is a happy man. A holder of the Stanislas medal, second degree, himself, a *teacher*, who, now, himself, labors to convey that selfsame "*ut consecutivum.*" And, granted, a person of some intelligence, yes—yes, but does happiness reside in that . . . ?

(*In the house, someone is playing the piano.*)

IRINA: As of tomorrow evening I need never again be subjected to that song. I need never again encounter Protopopov. That same Protopopov who came today, too, and who is out there in our parlor.

KULYGIN: Has the headmistress arrived?

IRINA: No.

KULYGIN: . . . no?

IRINA: . . . she's coming.

KULYGIN: Yes?

IRINA: Yes. She's been sent for. You know, it's been so lonely here. With Olga gone all day. So lonely. She's at the academy. She *lives* there. "The headmistress . . ." Busy all day. Important things. (*Pause.*) Important work. What do I have to do? Nothing to occupy me. Nothing. (*Pause.*) A hateful life. Yes. It is. My "room . . ." (*Pause.*) And I've decided this: if I am *destined* (*pause*) if it's *written* that I will live in Moscow . . . then I will do so. If It Is Not To *Be* (*pause*) then it was *not* so written. And it's fate. And nothing's to be done about it, it's God's will. It's true. That's what I thought. And what I have arrived at. (*Pause.*) Nikolai Lvovich asked me for my hand. He is a good man. And. As I *thought* of it, my soul *lightened*, my burden "grew light." A burden lifted, and I was, at once, I became "cheerful." And wanted to *work*. I wanted to "turn my hand" to some work. To something. But yesterday . . . (*Pause.*) Yesterday, something . . . (*Pause.*) Something "moved me from it." Something hov'ring over me . . .

CHEBUTYKIN: Disregard it.

NATALYA (*in the window*): The headmistress . . .

KULYGIN: The headmistress has arrived.

(KULYGIN *goes into the house with* IRINA.)

CHEBUTYKIN (*reads the paper, sings softly*): "Tra traaa. Upon this Stone I sit . . ."

(MASHA *approaches. In the background,* ANDREI *is wheeling the baby carriage.*)

MASHA: And there he is. Sitting.

CHEBUTYKIN: So what?

MASHA: What?

CHEBUTYKIN: What of it?

MASHA: Nothing.

CHEBUTYKIN: Well, then.

MASHA: Did you love my mother?

CHEBUTYKIN: Yes. I loved her very much.

MASHA: Did she love you? (*Pause.*)

CHEBUTYKIN: . . . it was so long ago.

MASHA: And is my Very Own One here? That's how our
old cook used to speak of her policeman. "My Very
Own *One*." S'my very own one here?

CHEBUTYKIN: He isn't here yet.

MASHA: When happiness is given to you only in *install-
ments*, do you know? In little "bits"—and then not even
that, you *coarsen*. Did you know that? And you become
mean. You become terribly small. As I have. And
there's our Andrei. Darling of Our Hopes. Our brother.
For the Multitudes Subscribed to Raise a Bell. And
Capital and Labor were expended on it. On the bell.
But in the *raising* of it, it fell. And it shattered. (*Pause.*)
No notice. (*Pause.*) No reason. (*Pause.*) And so it is with
Andrei. Little Modern Fable.

ANDREI: When will we have quiet in the house . . . the
noise . . .

CHEBUTYKIN: There will be quiet soon. (*Looks at his watch.*)
My antique repeated. Half hour. Quarter hour . . .
(*Pause.*) The "hour," of course . . . the first, the fifth, and
seventh companies embark at one exactly. (*Pause.*) And,
then, I go tomorrow.

ANDREI: And go until.

CHEBUTYKIN: Until?

ANDREI: Forever?

CHEBUTYKIN: Forever. Can't say. Might return. One year. Don't know. S'all one, really.

(*Somewhere, far off, sound of a harp and violin.*)

ANDREI: . . . the town.

CHEBUTYKIN: . . . yes?

ANDREI: Will be like an empty *tin*. There was some "to-do" at the theatre yesterday. Everyone's talking of it in short-hand. I missed it.

CHEBUTYKIN: . . . did you.

ANDREI: What was it?

CHEBUTYKIN: Nothing. Some foolishness.

ANDREI: Yes.

CHEBUTYKIN: Solyony goading the baron. (*Pause.*) The baron felt his "honor" had been . . . one thing led to the next, and Solyony felt obliged to *challenge* him.

ANDREI: Challenge the baron . . . ?

CHEBUTYKIN: That's right.

MASHA: To a duel?

CHEBUTYKIN (*looking at his watch*): Yes. I would think, just about *now*. Half past. The Birch Grove. (*Points out the window.*) "The Birch Grove over the River." Just make it out. (*Makes shooting gestures.*) Eight. Nine. Ten! Kapang! Solyony thinks he's Lermontov. Bad verse. The whole of him. Well. Fun is fun, but this is his third duel.

MASHA: His third?

CHEBUTYKIN: Yes.

MASHA: Whose?

CHEBUTYKIN: Solyony.

MASHA: And the baron?

CHEBUTYKIN: The baron.

MASHA: Yes.

CHEBUTYKIN: What?

MASHA: No. "It's." I can't . . . haven't . . . no, I haven't finally sorted it out, but, no, it shouldn't be allowed.

CHEBUTYKIN: It shouldn't.

MASHA: He might *kill* him. Or . . . he might "wound" him . . .

CHEBUTYKIN: Who?

MASHA: . . . the baron.

CHEBUTYKIN: Well. The baron's a good man. But one *baron* more or less I mean, let's not "sentimentalize" it. (*Pause.*) Let them fight.

(*A shout offstage.*)

Svortzoff. His second.

MASHA: Where is he?

CHEBUTYKIN: In the boat.

ANDREI: It is my opinion that to aid in any way the prog-ress of a duel, or to *countenance* it, even as a doctor . . .

CHEBUTYKIN: . . . Yes?

ANDREI: Is wrong.

CHEBUTYKIN: Yes. Well, no. It only *seems* so. For we do not abet it. We are not "of" it. (*Pause.*) We are not there. Nothing is there. We do not exist. There is no one *thinking* this. It's all just "seeming." (*Pause.*)

MASHA: And so they talk. One day, the *next* day. Always. Fall to winter. Soon it will snow, and this *talk*. No. I'm not going in the house. I'm not coming in. You'll tell me when Vershinin comes. (*Looks up.*) "The birds of Passage." Migratory birds. Moving already. Lucky ones. (*Exits.*)

ANDREI: The house empties itself. The garrison is gone. The sisters will go. *You'll* go. I'll be left alone.

CHEBUTYKIN: And your wife?

(*Enter* FERAPONT, *carrying papers.*)

ANDREI: A wife is a wife.

CHEBUTYKIN: And how is that?

ANDREI: A decent. Kind, all of the adjectives . . . a woman, you know . . . but . . . but . . . I feel. There is something in her. That. For want of a better word . . . (*Pause.*) You know, I so treasure, if I may, the opportunity to be open with you. You are the only one I truly can be frank with. (*Pause.*) I love my wife. I do. But at times, I feel that she brings me to a level where . . . where all I can feel is *revulsion*. And I feel *hatred* for her. And for her petty *ways*. I do. And her *vulgarity*. And *selfishness* passing as reason. And I don't understand. And I don't remember . . . how it was, how, I came to "love" her, or . . .

CHEBUTYKIN (*rising*): Waaal. (*Pause.*) My friend. I'm off tomorrow. And it's unlikely that we will meet again. And so, I'm going to give you some advice. (*Pause.*) Get your hat. Pick up your walking stick. Go out and walk. Never come back. Never *look* back. And the farther off you walk, the better.

> (SOLYONY *turns, crosses the back of the stage with his seconds. He sees* CHEBUTYKIN, *stops. The seconds go on.*)

SOLYONY: Doctor. Half past twelve. It's time.

> (SOLYONY *greets* ANDREI.)

CHEBUTYKIN: One moment. (*Sighs.*) Lord, I'm sick of it all. I'm sick of you all. (*To* ANDREI:) If they ask for me, you'll say, I've just . . . (*Gestures, as if to say, "Gone off for a moment."*)

SOLYONY: "And hardly had he cried 'alack'
Before the bear was on his back!"
And what is *your* trouble, Old Man?

CHEBUTYKIN: Mmm.

SOLYONY: How *are* you this fine day?

CHEBUTYKIN: . . . excuse me.

SOLYONY: No, no, no, he frets himself for nothing. I won't *hurt* him. I may *wing* him—like a *woodcock*, eh, to "bring him *down* . . ." (*He sprinkles eau de cologne on his hands.*) That's one whole bottle gone today. Hands smell of *death*. "And he, rebellious seeks the Tempest. As though in the Storm he could find Peace . . ."

CHEBUTYKIN: And "hardly had he cried 'alack' before the bear was on his back." (*Exits with* SOLYONY.)

(*Shouts of* Coo-eeeee *and* Yoohoo *are heard. Enter* FERAPONT *and* ANDREI.)

FERAPONT: . . . Papers to sign. The papers must be signed.

ANDREI: No, please . . . Leave me alone . . . Please . . . *No.* (*He goes off with the baby carriage.*)

FERAPONT: Well, that's what papers are *for.* What are they for, if not to be signed . . . ? (Exits).

(*Enter* TUZENBACH *and* IRINA; KULYGIN *walks across the stage, shouting* Coo-eeeee, Masha, Coo-eeeee.)

TUZENBACH: Well. There's the only one in town is glad the garrison is off.

IRINA: The town will be empty now.

TUZENBACH: Darling. I'll be back soon.

IRINA: Where are you going?

TUZENBACH: Just into town. To see my friends off.

IRINA: Is that true?

TUZENBACH: Yes.

IRINA: No. It's not. *Nikolai.* What was it happened yesterday?

TUZENBACH: . . . yesterday?

IRINA: In front of the theatre.

TUZENBACH: My darling. My darling. I'll be back. One hour. (*He kisses her.*) My dearest one. I've worshiped you for these five years. Each time I see you. It's a revelation. I *remember* you as beautiful, and then we meet, and you are *always* more beautiful than I remember. It doesn't change. It only grows stronger. I feel like I'm falling. I do. When I look at you. And *tomorrow:* I'll take you away. To be mine. To be with me. How can that be? That happiness? All my dreams. Can that be? Everything but the one thing: that you don't love me.

IRINA: How can I? (*Pause.*) I cannot "feel" it. How can one force oneself? I told you. I will be your wife. And I will serve you. Obediently. And faithfully. But if I do not love you, how am I to love? How??? . . . (*She weeps.*) Tell me that. Not once in my life. Not once. And I long for it. And I *dream* of it. My soul is a jewelry box. And they've lost the key . . . what is it?

TUZENBACH: What is it? It's *you.* I know what you're saying. I *feel* it. All night. And I don't sleep. And I *wake.* And I am thinking of that lost, as you say, of that "lost key," and don't you think that it *torments* me? Say something to me. (*Pause.*) I said say something.

IRINA: What?

TUZENBACH: What? Anything. I'm sorry. Say something.

IRINA: I don't know what to say.

TUZENBACH (*sighs*): Isn't it funny. How these things begin? And yet we go on . . . *seeing* them. And can't stop ourselves. Going on.

IRINA: What are you talking about?

TUZENBACH: No. You're right. Today . . . today is a day to be *glad.* Or be *content.* Or see the trees around us, you know? Our *maples*. Our *birth* trees. Each with its own life. Isn't it? As if they were *watching* us. They are so permanent. *We're* so . . . but it's as if to live near them we're to have an education. (*A shout offstage.*) I must go on. (*Pause.*) That one *there* . . . you see? It's dead. But it still sways when the wind blows. Just like the others. As it seems to me, if *I* would die, that something would go on. In some way. Do you see? (*Pause. He kisses her hand.*) Darling. Farewell. The papers you gave me are in my desk.

IRINA: I'll come with you.

TUZENBACH: No. No. *Irina* . . .

IRINA: Yes. What is it?

TUZENBACH: I. Didn't get my coffee today. They forgot to make it. Would you tell them that. (*Exits.*)

FERAPONT (*entering*): Andrei Sergeyevich. (*Pause.*) These papers aren't mine. They are "official" papers. From the *bureau*. They aren't mine . . . they aren't *my* papers.

ANDREI: What did I do with my life? I was young. I was bright and clever. Future before me. Full of Joy. I saw it. How could it be otherwise? And then it was past. Just young, just begun to live. And become old. Dull. Useless. Carping. Bitter. Failed. (*Pause.*) Fools. Cheated miserable fools. (*Pause.*) We have one hundred thousand people in this town. And not one fit to emulate. Or to admire. They *eat*. They *breed*. They *die*. They grow stupid from boredom. They drink and gamble, and they cheat at cards. The women cuckold the men, who pretend not to know. The children are raised in this sewer of hypocrisy. (*To* FERAPONT:) What do you want?

FERAPONT: What? *Papers* to sign.

ANDREI: You make me want to die. (FERAPONT *hands him the papers.*)

FERAPONT: The porter from the bureau told me in Petersburg this winter they had two hundred degrees of frost.

ANDREI: The present nauseates me. I think of the future, and I feel clean. (*Pause.*) Thinking of the future. (*Pause.*) I see: a life without drink, without the *stench* of bad cooking, without after-dinner naps . . . a life free of parasites, and . . .

FERAPONT: Two thousand people froze. They did. In Petersburg. Hmm. Or Moscow.

ANDREI: Oh, Lord.

NATALYA (*in the window*): Could we please keep our voices down? Who is . . . ? Andriushka? Is that you? You'll wake the baby. *Il ne faut pas faire de bruit, la Sofie est dormée déjà. Vous êtes un ours.* No. If you want to shout, give the *child* and the *carriage* to someone else. Ferapont.

FERAPONT: Madame?

NATALYA: Take the carriage from the master.

FERAPONT: Yes, Madame.

ANDREI: But I'm talking quietly.

NATALYA (*behind the window, talking to her boy*): Bobik . . . *Bad* Bobik. Yes, "nonobedient . . ."

ANDREI (*glancing through the papers*): Fine, fine, alright. I'll glance through them. I'll *sign* them, and then you take them back to the Board. *Fine.*

(Goes into the house reading the papers. FERAPONT *pushes the carriage to the back of the garden.)*

NATALYA *(behind the window)*: *Bobik.* Yes! What's your mama's name? *Bobik.* What's . . . yes. What's your mama's name? And who is that? Your aunt. *Olga.* Can you say her name? *Olga.* Yeesss . . .

(Wandering musicians play on violin and harp. VERSHININ, OLGA, *and* ANFISA *come out of the house and listen for a moment.* IRINA *approaches.)*

OLGA: Our garden is a turnpike. Everyone cuts through it. *Nanny.*

ANFISA: . . . my dear.

OLGA: Give the musicians something.

ANFISA *(gives money to the musicians)*: Go with God. Hard life. *(Pause.)* Don't play music in the streets if you're not hungry. *(To* IRINA:*)* My little one. What a life. What a life you've given me. At the *academy.* My own *apartment.* With my Oliushka. The Lord has vouchsafed to me. Comfort in my last years. And not since I was born, black as I am with Sin, have I enjoyed such comfort. Apartment, paid for by the government. My own *alcove.* My own *bed.* It costs me *nothing* . . . I wake in the night and pray, and in my prayer is this: "No one, mother of God, is happier than me."

VERSHININ *(glancing at his watch)*: Olga Sergeyevna. I must go. I wish you everything . . . everything that . . . where is Maria Sergeyevna?

IRINA: Somewhere in the garden. Shall I get her?

VERSHININ: If you would. (*Looks at his watch.*) Thank you.

ANFISA: *I'll* find her. (*Exits with* IRINA.) Mashenka! Mashenka! chick, chick, chick, chick . . .

VERSHININ: Everything must end. (*Pause.*) And now we are parting. The town gave us, you could call it, a "breakfast." The mayor made a speech. Champagne. My soul was here with you. (*Pause.*) I've, you know, I've grown used to you.

OLGA: Will we meet again?

VERSHININ: I would not think so. (*Pause.*) My wife will be staying on another month . . .

OLGA: . . . yes.

VERSHININ: If she, or the little ones should *need* something . . .

OLGA: Of course. Of course. I promise you. (*Pause.*) Tomorrow there won't be one uniform in the whole town. (*Pause.*) A memory. And the new life begins. And. (*Pause.*) It never falls out our way. Does it? The way we planned. (*Pause.*) I didn't want to be headmistress. Here I am. Not in Moscow. Here . . .

VERSHININ: Well. (*Pause.*) I thank you. For everything. (*Pause.*) Thank you. And, please, know of my deep respect for you, and that . . . one moment that I will remember you.

OLGA: Oh, where is *Masha*, then . . . ?

VERSHININ: And what else can I say. By the way of farewell? What have we left unsaid? What insights of philosophy? Hmm. "Life is Hard." Does that do it? It seems to us dull. Dull and repetitious. Without hope. And yet, as we live it, *if we wish*, it becomes clearer.

(*Looks at his watch.*) So much strife. Wars. Campaigns, victories. But we've left that now. Haven't we? Left it behind. A void. Now. All of that energy. For what? And how shall we fill it? That new thing? Of course we're seeking it. The educated. Seeking *labor.* Labor. Seeking "insight" . . . (*Looks at his watch.*) I must go.

OLGA: Here she is.

    (*Enter* MASHA.)

VERSHININ: I've come to say goodbye.

    (OLGA *walks away a little. Pause.*)

MASHA: Farewell. (*Beat. A prolonged kiss.*)

    (OLGA *clears her throat. They look to her for a moment.* MASHA *sobs.*)

VERSHININ: Write me. Don't forget me. Don't forget me. (*He kisses Olga's hands. Embraces* MASHA *again.*) Don't forget me. (*Exits.*)

    (*Pause.*)

OLGA: Shhhh. Masha. Shhhh, now. Come now, darling . . .

    (*Enter* KULYGIN.)

KULYGIN: It's alright. Let her cry. No. No. (*Pause.*) Masha. You're my wife. My good, kind Masha. My wife. And I reproach you with *nothing.* Do you hear me? *Nothing.* And I am content. (*To* OLGA:) As you will witness.

(*To* MASHA:) We'll begin again. And no one will say one word of what has occurred. Not a word, not a *reference* . . .

MASHA: . . . I'm going mad . . .

OLGA: Calm yourself, Masha. Please. Calm yourself. Get her some water.

MASHA: I don't need it.

KULYGIN: No. She doesn't need it. She's no longer crying. No.

(*Distant sound of a shot.*)

MASHA: Why should I need anything. My life is finished. Really. I'll be calm. In just a moment. You must forgive me. My head is spinning now. My *thoughts* . . .

(*Enter* IRINA.)

OLGA: Shhh. Masha. That's a clever girl. You calm yourself now. Come up to my room.

MASHA: No I will *not*. I'm not going in there. And I'm not going in the house. No.

IRINA: Alright, then. We'll sit here. We'll be silent. (*Pause.*) I'm off tomorrow, you know.

KULYGIN: I can make myself into the German master. Would you like to see it? (*Puts on false moustache and beard. Postures.*) I took them yesterday off a boy in the second form.

MASHA: You look like him.

OLGA: You look exactly like him!

(MASHA *weeps*.)

KULYGIN: Funny, those boys.

IRINA: Come, Masha.

KULYGIN (*to himself*): . . . I look so much like him.

(*Enter* NATALYA.)

NATALYA (*to the maid*): Take Bobik. Andrei Sergeyevich can
give him a ride. A *constant* drain, children. (*Pause*.) The
watchfulness! Irina. Leaving us tomorrow. What a pity.
Stay on one more week. (*Sees* KULYGIN, *cries out, then
laughs*.) You *frightened* me, you "*Prussian*." (*To* IRINA:)
No, I've become *used* to you. And now you're torn away.
I'll put Andrei into your room. He can play his music in
there. And little Sofie in *his* room, that angel. Angel
mine. My darling, who looked at me this morning with
such a *look*, which *did* speak volumes; and she said
"*mama*" (*Pause*.) ". . . Mama . . ."

KULYGIN: You're blessed with a fine child.

NATALYA: Well. Then. Tomorrow. That means I shall be
alone. (*Sighs*.) I'm going to take the fir trees down. The
whole lane of them. Then the maple there. It looks so
vulgar in the evening. (*To* IRINA:) Darling: that belt
doesn't suit you in the least. It wants something a little
less "pronounced." And over there, what do you think?
A bed of *flowers*. And the scent . . . from the bed of
flowers. (*To maid, pointing at the bench:*) Why is this fork
here? (*Shouts*.) Why is there a *fork* lying on the *bench*
here, please? (*Pause. She exits into the house*.) Why is

there a *fork* on the *bench* out here, I'm asking. (*Pause.*)
No . . . ?

KULYGIN: . . . and she is off.

(*Offstage, a march is being played. They listen.*)

OLGA: That's the last of the garrison.

(*Enter* CHEBUTYKIN.)

MASHA: Our people are going away. (*Pause.*) Our Family.
(*Pause.*) Well. (*Pause.*) A pleasant journey. (*To* KULYGIN:)
Shall we go? Where's my hat?

KULYGIN: . . . put it in the house. Shall I go fetch it?

MASHA: Thank you.

OLGA: Yes. It's time.

CHEBUTYKIN: Olga Sergeyevna?

OLGA: Yes? (*Pause.*) What? (*Pause.*) What?

CHEBUTYKIN: It's . . .

OLGA: What is it?

CHEBUTYKIN: I don't know how to tell you.

OLGA: How to tell me what? (*Pause.*) No. It can't be. No.

CHEBUTYKIN: This day has killed me . . .

MASHA: What's happened?

OLGA (*embraces* IRINA): Irina . . . I . . . darling . . . darling . . .

IRINA: What? *All* of you . . . what?

CHEBUTYKIN: The baron was killed in the duel.

IRINA (*weeps*): Yes. I knew. I knew.

CHEBUTYKIN (*sits*): Oh, *God*. I am exhausted. (*Sighs.*) (*Pause. Takes out a newspaper, reads.*) . . . They'll cry it out a bit. (*Sings to himself softly.*) "Ta tumm ta tummm tummm tummm tummm. Upon this Stone I sit." And, finally, it's all one.

(*The sisters stand holding on to one another.*)

MASHA: Oh. Fine. Play the music. Play them off. Away they go. One of them forever. For good. And isn't it true that we are left here, looking at a life that we . . . we must "create," and . . . (*Pause.*)

IRINA: In a time. Yes. In a time. It will be clear to us. What seems now to be *punishment* will be revealed. It will. And the meaning of suffering. Until then, what do we have but work? I will work. In the school. I'll give my life to those who may *profit* from it. (*Pause.*) The autumn passes. Winter comes. And the snow covers everything. And I'll be working . . .

OLGA: . . . the music plays so *brightly*. (*Pause.*) Time passes. Everything passes. We pass. We were only here for a little while. Too little to know. How can we help but think our suffering may be *transfigured*. To some good. For those who follow us? Who may remember us. Who may *bless* us. Or bless our memory. We who are living now. My darlings. Oh. Dear sisters.

(*Music grows softer and softer.* KULYGIN *enters bringing Masha's hat.* ANDREI *wheels the baby carriage.*)

... oh. My dears. The music plays so brightly. You would think, in just a little while, that we . . .

CHEBUTYKIN (*reading his paper, sings*): "Ta dummm, ta dummm, ta dummm, ta dummm . . . Upon this Stone I sit . . ." (*Sighs.*) *Oh* yes . . .

OLGA: If only we knew. If only we *knew* . . .